Schooling for Refugee Children

Schooling for Refugee Children

A social justice perspective informed by children from Syria

Eleanore Hargreaves, Brian Lally, Bassel Akar,
Jumana al-Waeli and Jasmine Costello

First published in 2024 by
UCL Press
University College London
Gower Street
London WC1E 6BT

Available to download free: www.uclpress.co.uk

ISBN: 978-1-80008-681-4 (Hbk)
ISBN: 978-1-80008-682-1 (Pbk)
ISBN: 978-1-80008-683-8 (PDF)
ISBN: 978-1-80008-684-5 (epub)
DOI: https://doi.org/10.14324/111.9781800086838

This book is dedicated to all children who have been displaced by war.

كم منزل في الأرض يألفه الفتى، و حنينه أبدا لأول منزل
We can inhabit many homes, but we will forever yearn
for our first home.

Abu Tammam (803–845)

Contents

List of figures and tables

Figures

Table

Abbreviations

BBC	British Broadcasting Corporation
CERD	Centre for Educational Research and Development, Lebanon
DfE	Department for Education, UK
DfES	Department for Education and Skills, UK
ICESCR	International Covenant on Economic, Social and Cultural Rights
INEE	Inter-agency Network for Education in Emergencies
LBP	Lebanese Pounds
LMIC	Low- to middle-income country
MAPs	Multi-Aid Programs
MEHE	Ministry of Education and Higher Education, Lebanon
NGO	Non-governmental organisation
RACE	Reaching All Children with Education
UN	United Nations
UNCRC	United Nations Convention on the Rights of the Child
UNHCR	United Nations High Commissioner for Refugees
UNICEF	United Nations Children's Fund
UNISCE	United Nations International Standard Classification of Education

Authors' note on pictures of children's writing

At the start of all the chapters, we present pieces of writing produced by some of the children who attended our research workshops. Their words were addressed to their teachers in Arabic, as expressed also in writing during the workshops (and later translated by one of our authors). The text of this book is interspersed with drawings from children attending the MAPs schools.

Foreword

As an educator and as a researcher, I am always hungry to know more about processes. How does something happen, why does it happen, and how is it experienced? This book has a welcome focus on processes that are enacted, experienced, and analysed by children, teachers, and researchers. As a reader, I appreciate the purposeful scaffolding of the book that allows me to see and better understand how decisions were made and why, in the context of relationships with children and with teachers, and of co-authorship among the researchers. This transparency of process creates a bridge, opening opportunities for the reader not only to see, listen to, and learn from the 45 Syrian children featured in this study but also to prompt greater understanding of our own processes as well: how we learn, how we teach, and how we research.

I want to focus on four particular elements of this approach and the opportunities they provide for the field of refugee education: looking, listening, learning and living-out.

Looking. Children's drawings fill this book with representations of their experiences, feelings, and sense-making. As readers, we are invited to look carefully and to actively see what representation might look like when space is held open and trust is felt for children to share their ideas. As the authors document, this space and trust can be rare for refugee children to experience and immensely challenging and sometimes risky for teachers to create.

Listening. As a research tool, the authors present listening as an ethical commitment – to the children they work with, to their teachers, and to each other as professionals. Through this commitment, they also document listening as a central pedagogical tool that the Syrian children in their study point to – a tool with which possibilities for representation and participation in schools can be created. Children's power over how learning happens in school depends on whether, and how, their teachers listen to them, try to understand what they are hearing, and create space for acting on the needs and desires expressed.

Learning. By engaging children, their teachers, themselves as researchers, and us as readers, the authors of this book prompt us to re-examine the purposes of education – specifically, refugee education – in light of what we learn from each other through this looking and listening. This commitment to shared learning is apparent not only in the approach to research but also in the outcome of this research, a book that is being made widely available via Open Access. I read it as both a commitment to and an invitation into conversation and on-going engagement.

Living-out. Many a time, I read about a classroom or a school or a teacher and I think to myself, 'I would love to be able to do that, to create that, to be that.' I often feel stymied, though, in the gulf between my current reality and my aspirations. I need explanations of the processes of how a classroom came to be as it is, of why a school has certain policies, of the thinking a teacher goes through in making pedagogical decisions, of how children make sense of their experiences in these classrooms and schools, and with these teachers. In *Schooling for Refugee Children*, the authors' deep commitment to looking and listening with children and teachers and to learning through documenting, analysing and sharing these processes provides concrete examples of *how* children and teachers shape their school experiences toward practices of representation and parity of participation, driven by the goals of social justice.

Sarah Dryden-Peterson
Associate Professor
Harvard Graduate School of Education
Cambridge, Massachusetts

Acknowledgements

We would like to acknowledge all the children it has been our privilege to get to know and work with in the preparation of this book, as well as the committed teachers, support staff and NGO personnel who work in such challenging circumstances to do their best for the children in their care. In particular, we thank all those at Multi-Aid Programs (MAPs) who made our work not only possible but also personally transformative. We would also like to thank the team and children at Relief and Reconciliation for Syria, for facilitating our research in their non-formal education provision. In addition, we thank Annelise Anderson for her contributions.

We, as individual authors, acknowledge each other's rich and generous contributions during the process of producing this book.

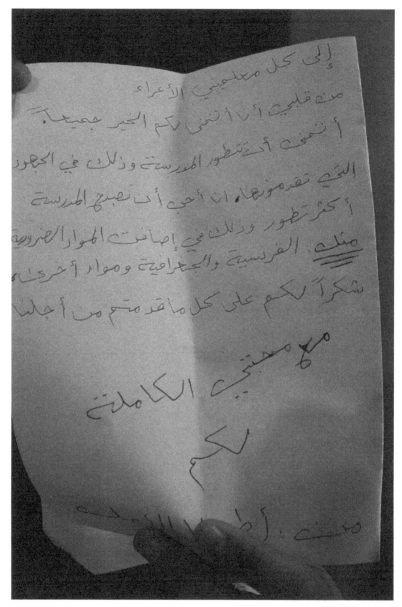

Figure 1.1   A MAPs pupil's letter to their teacher. © The authors.

To all my dear teachers,
I wish you all the best, from my heart.
I hope that the school improves by the efforts you are putting into it.
Thank you for everything you did for us.
With my great love to you,

Child of Hope from MAPs

1
Purposes of representing children's experiences

Raghida's story

I am a Syrian girl who was forced to migrate out of my country. My name is Raghida. I am 14 years old, born on the 4th of January 2005. I was a little girl when war started devastating my country. I left Syria when I was 7 years old; and I came to Lebanon as my grandmother and aunt were already living here. When we came to Lebanon, I went with my family to live in a camp for Syrian refugees, and we lived there for 2 years. One day, the owner of the camp came at 6 pm, and told everyone in the camp: 'You should all leave the camp by 2 pm tomorrow.' The next day, my father and my aunt started looking for a place. It was raining heavily. The man who owned the camp came and made everyone leave in 2 hours; so, we started moving our stuff in the rain to the new place. After two weeks, another man came to see us and asked us, along with the people who lived in the previous camp, to go with him to another camp and live there; thus, we went there, and we have been living in [the second] camp for 5 years now. I live with my family, which consists of my mum, my dad, two sisters and one brother. Across from this camp, there is a school in which my siblings and I are enrolled. I studied in this school from Grade 2 to Grade 6 [ages 8 to 12]. In the school, there were wonderful teachers. The school was called: the School of Hope, Sawasia. Teachers were kind to us and they treated us like they treat their own children or siblings. The headteacher's name was Wisam; he was a great, understanding and respectful headteacher.

This book examines the social justice of – and through – schooling for children like Raghida,[1] who, because of war, are forced to leave the home they knew, where they felt safe, where they belonged, and take refuge in another country. Globally, as of 2022, some 35.3 million people were counted as refugees, with 1.9 million born as refugees between 2018 and 2022. Of the global total in 2022, more than 7.6 million children were aged between 5 and 17 years (UNHCR, 2023). We focus on the refugees who left Syria after the crisis that began in 2011. The Syrian conflict that erupted in that year was far from being over by the beginning of the main research project that we conducted in 2019 and that guided the work in this book. During that crisis, an estimated 11 million people were forced to leave their communities in Syria (UNOCHA, 2016). The Government of Lebanon estimated that, as of November 2019, at least 1.5 million Syrian citizens were seeking refuge in Lebanon (UNHCR, 2020a). Raghida and her family were among these citizens. She found refuge in the Multi-Aid Programs (MAPs) community in Beqaa (sometimes spelt Bekaa), Lebanon.

Our interest in working with Syrian refugee children stems from our fundamental belief that all children have the right to a socially just education. From this perspective, schooling would allow them to develop their capacities; respond to their needs; ensure their right to participate on a par with all other children; and support their right to make their needs heard. Many disadvantaged children, including Syrian refugee children, are prevented from exercising these fundamental rights, especially those in Lebanese camps and temporary settlements. Furthermore, the knowledge field of education for refugees relies heavily on context- and culture-specific circumstances such as the political, geographical, social, legal and economic distances between the host country and the displaced country (Anderson et al., 2004). Hence, we approach the work in this book with profound respect for the highly contextualised and nuanced narratives of Syrian refugee children at particular sites in Lebanon and England. It is against this backdrop that we conducted three projects, each one corresponding to a case study – presented later in this book – that offered a platform for forcibly displaced and disadvantaged Syrian refugee children in their respective contexts in the two aforementioned countries to share their stories and represent their different educational experiences. By communicating and examining the children's representations, we embody an unwavering commitment to safeguarding the dignity of forcibly displaced children. Moreover, the children exercise their right to parity of participation in social life by representing their own needs, views and preferences in safety.

Before introducing the three case studies, we will briefly describe the status of Syrian children who fled the war in Syria to neighbouring countries, with a focus on Lebanon.

The status of Syrian refugee children in Lebanon

Most refugees escaping the armed conflict in Syria fled to countries in the region – in particular, the 'big five' hosting countries of Turkey, Lebanon, Jordan, Iraq and Egypt. Figures 1.2 and 1.3 present memories of escaping the war depicted by two Syrian children at an education centre run by MAPs, a Lebanese non-governmental organisation (NGO). A major part of our research for this book concentrated on Lebanon. The unprecedented transient influx of Syrian refugees accounted for a population increase of approximately 25 per cent within Lebanon's borders (Culbertson & Louay, 2015, p. ix). United Nations (UN) registration data (UNICEF, 2016a) indicate that, in 2016, over half a million Syrian refugees in Lebanon were children between the ages of 3 and 18.

The sheer volume alone represented an enormous challenge to the systems and services necessary to meet the needs of this vulnerable population, including, of course, shelter, clean water and education.

Figure 1.2 'Escaping the war' by a Syrian refugee pupil at a MAPs education centre. © The authors.

Figure 1.3 'My journey to Lebanon' by a pupil at MAPs. © The authors.

However, public services were already seen as limited or stretched even before the flood of refugees into the country. For example, education in Lebanon prior to the crisis struggled to break out of political gridlock over curricular reform (Frayha, 2010) and suffered from a lack of qualified practitioners in its public schools (El-Amine, 2004; MEHE, 2010).

During the influx, state-school leaders admitting Syrian refugee children into their centres reportedly struggled with unclear operational procedures, limited classroom size, and a shortage of personnel qualified to teach and support forcibly displaced children with limited literacy (Örücü, Arar & Mahfouz, 2021). Furthermore, statistics consistently showed that only 30 per cent of Lebanese children attended state schools rather than private schools (CERD, 2014; 2019), demonstrating the generalised low level of confidence in the quality of state education, even prior to the successive influxes of refugees.

The settlement of Syrian refugees in Lebanon is neither evenly spread across the country nor stable, largely because of the Lebanese Government's anti-settlement discourse. For the purposes of this book, we use the word 'camp' to refer to informal tented settlements where the least economically advantaged live – among them, the refugee Syrian community. The most significant concentration of refugees in these informal camps has been in the northern region and in the Beqaa Valley, to the east of the country (see Figure 1.4). Both of these areas were noted

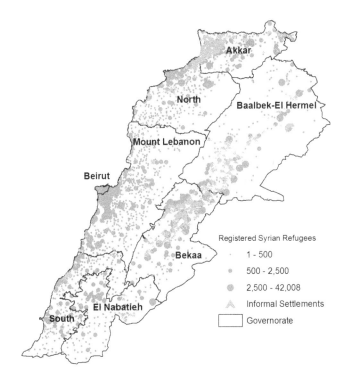

Figure 1.4 Distribution of Syrian refugees in Lebanon.
Source: UNHCR, 2015, p. 3

by UNHCR (2015) as already facing difficulties around service provision and significant socio-economic challenges prior to the Syrian crisis.

Furthermore, under a policy decision by the Lebanese Government, neither international agencies nor NGOs are permitted to establish official camps for the Syrian refugees, with the associated formal services such as education (UNHCR, 2015). In contrast, in other host countries, fundamental services such as education and health are typically provided, such as in the case of Colombia for refugees from Venezuela and Kenya for incoming communities from South Sudan, Ethiopia and Somalia. Lebanon's resistance to settling Syrian refugees largely stems from the association between settling Palestinian refugees in the 1950s and 1960s and the Lebanese Civil War (1975–90) that involved armed conflict between Palestinian armed groups and the Israeli army (Kelly, 2017). Furthermore, Lebanon is not a signatory to the UN 1951 Refugee Convention on the Status of Refugees or its related 1967

Protocol (IRC, 2016). The Lebanese Government maintains its resistance to signing this Convention partly because of the required *permanent* settlement of refugees. This has led to a situation in which voluntary responses to the need to host refugees surpass the efforts of far more stable countries (Janmyr, 2017).

The three case studies

Across our three case studies – two from Lebanon, one from England – we asked child refugees to represent their experiences, reflections and visions of schooling. We also asked what facilitated and what obstructed their experiences; and we encouraged their critiquing of current practices. The purpose of examining these three case studies is not to compare them with each other but to shed light on the different, yet closely related, experiences of disadvantaged and displaced children in countries of both temporary and permanent settlement. We also acknowledge that these studies are not representative of the perspectives of forcibly displaced children across the world. Clearly, contexts, needs and aspirations vary considerably. The aim of our research was to depict vividly the experiences and perspectives of three specific groups of children, not to seek to paint a representative picture of all forcibly displaced children. Throughout, however, we acknowledge that facilitating activities for refugee children – or, indeed, any children – to express and act upon their hopes and ideals around better learning is an exceptional approach in educational settings, generally, where it is rarely practised or attempted.

Our first case study (Chapter 4) is based on a collaborative research project in which the authors all participated in different capacities; hence, it occupies the largest share of the book. This project took place in Lebanon. Syrian children's accounts were collected during a three-day workshop at MAPs schools in Lebanon in May 2019, prior to the COVID-19 pandemic. Through a programme of carefully-tailored research activities, we investigated the children's respective representations of their personal journeys (see Figure 1.5) and schooling experiences in the context of social justice. Through participatory research activities with the children at the MAPs schools in the Beqaa Valley and Arsal, we sought to gain insights into what drove their experiences of schooling in temporary settlements; and we offer these insights to the discussion regarding the education of displaced children across global contexts.

Our second case study (Chapter 5) explores the perceptions of Syrian children in a school in London, England, where the young Syrians were settled permanently. The work with six Syrian children in the London school was carried out by Jumana al-Waeli as part of her doctoral research. Its theoretical framing was also applied to all our work in Lebanon; and, like our research in the MAPs schools, it aimed to explore how Syrian children represented their understandings of social justice as parity-of-participation in relation to their schooling, albeit in a different context that is mostly perceived as more stable. The study was conducted in 2019–20. It followed the journeys and day-to-day lives of young Syrians who, unlike their counterparts in Lebanon, had been granted the legal right, along with their families, to remain in the United Kingdom (UK). The children's narratives in this research stretched back to the start of the conflict in Syria and, thus, included their stories of displacement, their journeys toward refuge, and their post-settlement lives in London – of which school and its accompanying social life occupied a huge part. Mirroring the other two studies in this book, this case is concerned with the children's representations of their life-histories and accounts of day-to-day social and educational lives and encounters.

The third case study took place back in Lebanon but as part of non-formal education (NFE) initiatives, led by the NGO Relief & Reconciliation for Syria, designed to support Syrian refugee children

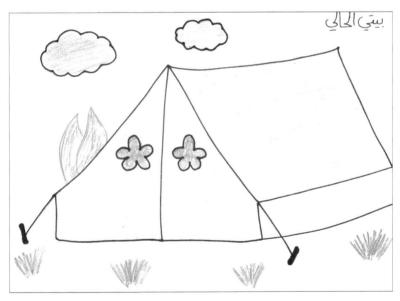

Figure 1.5 'My current home' by a Syrian refugee pupil at a MAPs education centre. © The authors.

in mainstream schooling. The NFE activities were especially significant during the time of study as they were the only education provision for the Syrian refugee children in that area during enforced school closures. Starting with the political uprisings in October 2019 and the subsequent COVID-19 pandemic, schools closed for two years – or even longer, in the case of the so-called 'second-shift' provision for Syrian refugee children that some state schools are charged with delivering. This is a second – briefer – running of the school day, often delivered by the same teachers as in the morning shift, catering almost exclusively to Syrian children (Akar, 2021). Observations and conversations were captured over four full-day visits during May and June 2021. We learned about the struggles not only of Syrian and Lebanese teachers endeavouring to support marginalised children in maintaining access to learning but also of a mainstream national education system that appeared to foster debilitating pedagogies for Lebanese and Syrians alike.

Introducing the chapters in this book

All the chapters that follow are co-authored, and all are guided by the theoretical frameworks of Nancy Fraser (2019) and Ravi Kohli (2011). This integration of frameworks was one that we developed collabora-tively, drawing on the PhD studies of two of the authors in the team as well as the existing work of the rest of the team (see the References section). In addition, throughout the book, we link the text to drawings made by refugee Syrian children at MAPs centres in Lebanon and to letters and messages they wrote to their teachers. By publishing this book through Open Access, it is our hope that these representations may be shared (and potentially acted on) globally.

In Chapter 1, we introduce the three case studies. We explain the purposes behind representing the displaced children's experiences, how and why these studies were conducted, and what guided them. In Chapter 2, we survey the theoretical frameworks of Nancy Fraser and Ravi Kohli, which provide the conceptual context within which we approached the data collected among the children. In Chapter 3, we explain how the legal parameters of primary education vary across nation-states. We also examine why primary education constitutes such a crucial developmental stage for vulnerable children and how it can address the social injustices that affect children vulnerable to conflict. We then critically review how international targets such as the Sustainable Development Goals have overlooked certain factors that limit global efforts toward an equitable and empowering primary education. The chapter ends with a description of primary education provision for Syrian refugee children in Lebanon.

Chapter 4, covering the first of the three case studies, starts by exploring how and why MAPs' education programme for displaced children came to be established and how its provision was contextualised for Lebanon and developed specifically for the community. It also outlines attempts by the Lebanese authorities, as well as international agencies, national NGOs and local, grass-roots civil society groups to meet the educational needs of the refugee community in Lebanon. The second part of the chapter presents the actual representations provided by the MAPs children in our 2019 research workshops, outlined earlier. It portrays expressions of love among MAPs children and their teachers; the children's thirst for learning; their capacity for hard work; and their social spirit of loyalty and honesty toward each other in achieving their ambitions.

Chapter 5 focuses on the second case study. London provides a different context for displaced Syrian children, whose search for safety and a sense of belonging contrasted with that of the MAPs children. While safety – both physical and legal – was precarious for the MAPs children, their sense of belonging in MAPs supported their perception of safety, which, in turn, allowed them to speak out more freely. The children in the London case study had a more concrete sense of safety in that they had been legally resettled in the UK. However, they expressed a weak sense of belonging in a London school, which appeared to contrast with their perception of safety and minimise their participation in the inclusive running of their schooling.

Chapter 6 presents the third case study, which draws on a series of visits to Relief & Reconciliation for Syria programmes. This NGO provides alternative NFE for Syrian refugee children in the North Lebanon governorate.

In Chapter 7, we return to the children at MAPs to explore how they managed to continue learning during the difficult era of the COVID-19 pandemic, which occurred after our original research. The pandemic coincided in Lebanon with a severe economic and political crisis that was further intensified by a massive explosion in the Beirut port area in 2020. The data described in this chapter draw on Brian Lally's doctoral research as well as additional interviews conducted specifically for this book. The chapter focuses particularly on teachers' attempts to act on the children's expressions and requests in the context of this safe community of Syrian migrants.

To conclude this book, Chapter 8 brings together learnings about how primary schooling can better position forcibly displaced children as informed and empowered participants or citizens in a society, on a par with children from more stable families. Conversely, it also examines what can be learned from our findings regarding the potential for schooling to further *marginalise* such children. Looking forward, we reflect on the extent to which empowering pedagogies are feasible and applicable within mainstream education contexts affected by compounded conflicts and authoritarian-like education systems. Considering the current, well-established education systems that have institutionalised pedagogies based on strict hierarchies and knowledge transfer, we suggest transformations within the pedagogical culture to begin empowering forcibly displaced children.

As the authors of this book, it has been a great experience for us to prepare and write together. We invite our readers to enjoy the book as a whole, appreciating the many long discussions that emerged for us along the way. Our book reflects our diverse perspectives on displaced Syrian children's education in the context of social justice, contributed from diverse social and political contexts. It has been written in a purposefully collaborative way. We are a team of five authors from five different work contexts and four different countries, each of whom brought to this book their particular experiences and strengths. We come from a range of educational disciplines, including conflict studies, pedagogy, child development and social justice. Additionally, the research projects described here shared a vision of facilitating these children's representations as part of improving social justice in education. Since carrying out the original MAPs research, we have discussed and re-discussed many aspects of this book, learning from and with each other across the time it has taken us to complete it. From all angles, the aim of this book has been to provide a public-facing forum for the experiences of the children (and their teachers) to be heard, and to stimulate challenging, critical conversations and actions among our readers that can build further on those captured here.

Note

1 As with all children's names referred to in this book, 'Raghida' is a pseudonym.

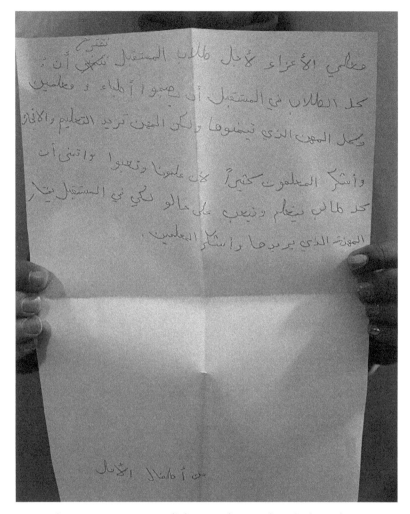

Figure 2.1 A MAPs pupil's letter to their teacher. © The authors.

My Dear Teachers

For the future students, we suggest that all the students in the future become doctors and teachers and all the careers they wish for. However, careers need education and achievement. I thank teachers very much because they taught us and made much effort, and I wish every student would learn and work hard so that in the future they can choose the career they want and I thank the teachers.

Child of Hope from MAPs

2
Social justice in displaced children's schooling: Children representing experiences

In this chapter, we draw on two frameworks that informed how we approached refugee children and their teachers and how we understood their representations of learning and better schooling. One is Nancy Fraser's concept of social justice for children. This provides a critical lens for exploring how displaced primary-school children perceive opportunities to be heard. The other framework is Ravi Kohli's notion of refugee children needing to establish feelings of safety, belonging and success. Working with forcibly displaced children under these two frameworks enabled us to better identify approaches to schooling that potentially empower refugee children to build a greater sense of security and to express their thoughts to teachers and peers on improving learning experiences.

Nancy Fraser's conceptualisation of social justice

Nancy Fraser (2008; 2019) conceptualises social justice as 'parity-of-participation'. Parity-of-participation speaks to the aim that all members of a society participate as equal peers in the construction of socio-political arrangements. According to Fraser's theory, the presence of social justice requires a deconstruction of traditional authoritarian power hierarchies, including those related to the nation-state, to ensure fair and equal participation in decision-making processes. This notion of levelling the playing field is particularly relevant to displaced people as it positions the individual as a citizen of the world rather than subject to the legal parameters of the nation-state. Indeed, given the global migration of people and the corresponding rapid increase in diversity, examining and defining social justice must extend beyond the political space of a nation-state to more universal understandings of equality of opportunity. Fraser (2018, pp. 92–3) argues for the following:

> ... a conception of justice that can – and should – be accepted by those with divergent conceptions of the good life ... everyone has an equal right to pursue social esteem under fair conditions of equal opportunity.

While we also reference others' writings on social justice, such as Amartya Sen's justice theory (1992, drawn on by Osler, 2016), we prioritise Fraser's work, given its specific focus on representation and its recent application to educational sites, including those in conflict areas (see, for example, Novelli et al., 2015).

Fraser's conceptualisation of social justice as parity-of-participation comprises three elements: 1) redistribution; 2) recognition; and 3) representation. These are represented in Figure 2.2 (adapted from Fraser, 2008). To illustrate each, Olson (2008, cited in Power, 2012) associates redistribution with fair economic participation, recognition with a validated expression of culture, and representation with participation in the political sphere. The three dimensions of social justice are also interdependent. Fraser (2018, p. 94) explains that, for representative (that is, the third aspect, political) justice to be practised, wealth and status must also be fairly distributed:

> The distribution of material resources must be such as to ensure participants' independence and voice ... Precluded, therefore, are social arrangements that institutionalise deprivation, exploitation, and gross disparities in wealth, income, and leisure time, thereby denying some people the means and opportunities to interact with others as people.

In the domain of education in conflict-affected areas, Novelli et al. (2015) add 'reconciliation' as a fourth R to redistribution, recognition and representation. Reconciliation considers the causal factors of conflicts and potential pathways toward peacebuilding.

Initially, Fraser only conceptualised the first two obstacles to participatory parity: lack of fair distribution and lack of social recognition. People suffer distributive injustice (maldistribution) when they are prevented from participating fully by economic structures that deny them the resources they need to interact with others. Often, those

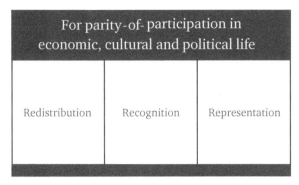

Figure 2.2 Nancy Fraser's three dimensions of social justice.
Source: Adapted from Fraser (2008).

from higher-income socio-economic classes have more direct access to resources. Also, people suffer status inequality (misrecognition) if they are prevented from interacting as peers by institutionalised hierarchies of cultural value that deny them requisite status. Later, Fraser added the third element, representation. This political dimension provides the conditions for facilitating the means for people's struggles over distribution and recognition. It defines the criteria of social belonging and membership and provides mechanisms by which everyone can play a role in resolving economic and cultural injustices (see Olson, 2008).

Representation

In this book, we focus particularly on political justice – representation – in education and schooling. The representation dimension encompasses two levels. The first pertains to social belonging, which includes defining the boundaries of who is included or excluded from the circle of those deemed to be entitled to negotiate and claim justice. The second level is concerned with the procedures that control the public processes of contestation, which is often embedded in a country's electoral voting system. Hence, parity-of-participation is strengthened through representation when 'interrogating silences and scrutinising invisibilities' (Keddie, 2012, p. 199). We drew on this idea when facilitating dialogic activities for the displaced Syrian schoolchildren who participated in our research.

When applied to an educational setting, the social justice aspect of equality of opportunity can only be maximised when those whom the education system serves are unconditionally and equally recognised and represented. Novelli et al. (2015) list ways to evaluate levels of representation in practice, which include:

- teachers, parents and children participating in making decisions in school governance activities
- extent to which policy reforms involve stakeholders' participation in design and decision-making on local, national and global levels
- political control or representation through fair administration of services
- diversity of stakeholders involved in local governance of services and decision-making processes (including families, communities and so on)
- extent to which the education services support fundamental freedoms.

Power (2012; see also Lundy, 2012; Tomasevski, 2001) argues that the politics of representation speaks more clearly to individual rights than do the other two aspects of social justice – redistribution and recognition. She also suggests that representation could include participation in the pursuit of individual projects as well as when working more broadly toward collective socio-political goals. We explore these aspects through the direct voices of the displaced children whose families had no safe place to call home in their nation-state of origin (Syria), seeking instead safety and a sense of belonging in the nation-state of residence (Lebanon or the UK). Across the case studies in this book, we ask what is needed to create the conditions necessary for refugee children to participate in representing their own experiences, their critiques and the personal requests emanating from these.

Community level versus social or global level

In an increasingly diverse and globalised world, the interconnections on the micro, meso and macro levels are critical to more fully understanding the presence and nature of social justice across all fields of human experience – or its absence. On the national or global level, injustices might occur when either a) the wider field dominates insensitively over individuals or b) the individual is left to seek justice without structured support. In terms of the first of these scenarios, several researchers have noted the tendency for national policies to be put in place that do not pay heed to, or indeed wilfully ignore, the diversities represented in a community, thereby failing to do justice to marginalised groups. For example, in England, McIntyre and Hall (2018) noted that the focus had moved from Every Child Matters (DfES, 2003) to paths of 'social mobility' tracked through progression and attainment measurements. This located refugees in England outside the main discourse, since their progress was only measured there if they had been in the country for at least two years. In Australia, Sidhu and Taylor (2007, p. 294) described how refugee children were mostly 'invisible' in education policy, as 'the practice of ignoring them or marginalising them in policy discourse places them at a significant disadvantage'.

This insensitivity to individuals' diversity is also played out by stigmatising policy depictions of refugee groups in ways that portray them as low-status humans. For example, it is acknowledged in some policy documents that refugees have high levels of resourcefulness and resilience due to their hard life-experiences. However, when education policy focuses on their victim or 'at-risk' nature, particularly the problematic process of their transition into a new setting, this can lead to 'essentialising and infantalising', which impedes their access to parity-of-participation (Keddie, 2012, p. 207) and is likely to quash their chances of success in the longer term (see Chapter 5).

Regarding the other scenario, whereby individuals are left to seek justice without structured support, Sidhu and Taylor (2007) noted a new global emphasis on partnership, which sounds collaborative but sometimes comes to mean that responsibility for attending to the wellbeing of disadvantaged individuals fell to local communities rather than being galvanised and organised by the state – as was the case of the MAPs schools (see Chapter 4). This can lead to an increase in separatism and group enclaving rather than trans-group interaction (Fraser, 2018). Indeed, both these tendencies can be seen in the Lebanese case with some even more divisive overtones (see Chapter 6).

Representation: A human right through active participation

Human rights underpin the three aspects of Fraser's conceptualisation of social justice. As Starkey (2012, p. 28) explains: 'With entitlement to dignity and recognition as a member of the human family comes entitlement to rights'. Article 2 of the UN Convention on the Rights of the Child (UNCRC) (United Nations, 1989) sets a foundation for parity of representation whereby children are not discriminated against, irrespective of their 'parents' or legal guardian's race, colour, sex, language, religion, political or other opinion, national, ethnic or social origin, property, disability, birth or other status'. Articles in the UNCRC also stipulate the right to participation through representation. For example, Article 12 of the UNCRC demands that children be accorded the opportunity to express their views and be encouraged to do so, while Article 13 focuses on the means for expressing views. The spirit of these two articles can be paraphrased as follows:

> **Article 12.** Respect for the views of the child: when adults are making decisions for children (for example, in schooling-related matters), to ensure that children can voice what they would like to see happening and can see how their views are taken into account.

> **Article 13.** Freedom of expression: the right of children to access and share information as long as it does not damage others; and the freedom to choose the means by which to express themselves … either orally, in writing or print, in the form of art, or through any other media of the child's choice.

We refer to the children's expressions of ideas, opinions and preferences as representations. Their representations must not only be listened to but also given due consideration and acted upon as appropriate by adults. The call for ensuring that children contribute to decision-making is also a foundational benchmark in the global Minimum Standards for Education (INEE, 2010). These standards encourage full and inclusive participation where any stakeholder – in this case, children – can contribute to how decisions are made and to the planning and implementation of educational activities. Furthermore, *all* children, not only the articulate and literate, must be able to express their views without 'fear of reprisal' (Rudduck & Flutter, 2004, p. 137). To avoid this fear, a sense of safety and belonging will need to characterise the learning environment.

The nature of the participation is also critical to ensuring that children's representations are also experiences of empowerment, engagement and influence. Lundy (2007, p. 931) describes how representation for social justice can be pursued by children when – with adult support – they are involved in three levels of decision-making: '(i) when decisions are being made which impact on individual pupils; (ii) when school and classroom policies are being developed; and (iii) when government policy/legislation on education is determined'. However, it is only high-quality participation among children that will ensure their dignified and meaningful representation. Drawing on the idea of degrees of participation, Arnstein's (1969) 'ladder of citizen participation', with its eight rungs of citizen power, suggests that, on the three lowest rungs of the participation ladder, children may take part in activities through forms of manipulation, decoration and tokenism, casting these as non-participation. On the middle rungs, he contends, they may be assigned roles or approached for consultations but, in both cases, are informed of the reasons for (and the outcomes of) their participation. At the higher levels of the ladder, Arnstein illustrates more agentic forms of participation where adults engage children in decision-making and where children initiate, lead and share decisions with adults.

By including children's perspectives in decisions regarding the design of their schooling, we create the necessary precursor to meeting their recognition and representation needs. Without such input, children cannot exercise full participation. This book (and the research process on which it is based) sought to provide a means for allowing displaced Syrian children to represent their own needs and views and, through its dissemination, to make these representations publicly available. Other parts of this book investigate the barriers that may obstruct the displaced child's exercising of this right.

Representation of expressed versus inferred needs

Listening to how children represent themselves in matters directly affecting them is essential to respecting their dignity as human beings. However, as Noddings (2005) so powerfully expressed, there is a danger that those responsible for young people will sometimes infer their needs rather than listen to the children's own expressed needs. There is a critical distinction between the two that often becomes conflated and overlooked by adults. According to Noddings (2005, p. 148) 'an expressed need comes from the cared-for; an inferred need comes from one trying to care'. While some inference will be necessary, a higher level of attending to expressed needs is certain to be more effective in providing for and responding appropriately to children, and also for allowing them to exercise their right to representation. The practice of adults *solely* using inferred needs to make decisions about schooling is rooted in authoritarian principles of power and control. This practice of inferring shows up in virtually every aspect of schooling and decisions concerning the curriculum and is also manifest in how children construct and express their ideas.

Noddings noted that most needs identified by educators were inferred and that most of these were 'inferred pre-actively' (2005, p. 149), meaning that the inferences are embedded into the curriculum before the educator has even met the children. When a critique of inferring needs is applied to an educational context, decisions about schooling must include hearing from those directly impacted by such decisions – the 'cared-for'. By opening up dialogue with children, we give them an opportunity not only to express their needs but also to express how they believe those needs might most effectively be met. In doing so, we open the possibility of provision becoming more effective in meeting those needs. In other words, it just might be that children know what works best for them. However, of course, the views of the 'cared-for' must also be analysed in light of rigorous research evidence too.

The case studies presented in this book demonstrate explicitly designed spaces for Syrian refugee children to represent their needs, to have these acknowledged and to have them directly acted upon. In this book, we use the word 'representation' rather than 'voice' since 'pupil voice' discourses are vulnerable to being defined in narrow terms at both extremes of the political spectrum, at least in the Global North. At one end, they can be characterised as progressive but misguided child-centred approaches that over-emphasise the role of children in knowing what is best for them. At the other end, a tokenistic approach regards pupil voice as a consideration that is fully addressed have expressed their opinions through devices such as surveys and school councils. Our conception of pupil voice rejects both extremes and considers children's representations and critiques of their experiences and their requests emanating from them as valuable, both as processes and as outcomes.

Kohli's theory of the need for safety, for a sense of belonging and for success

Inspired by McIntyre and Abrams (2021) and McIntyre and Neuhaus (2021), we adapt Ravi Kohli's (2011) central concept into a framework of three core needs:

- to feel safe
- to feel like one belongs
- to succeed.

The focus on these concepts of safety, belonging and success as needs enables us to more fully understand and act upon the social and educational experiences represented by displaced Syrians in schooling and align these with the discourse of social justice as proposed by Fraser. According to Kohli, these three needs are likely to be represented by displaced children. Kohli's theory embodies the assumption that, when social justice as parity-of-participation is in place, this provides the necessary conditions for young refugees to restore some form of ordinariness and regain a sense of home after settlement in a host country, be it temporary or permanent. In other words, when distribution, recognition and representation are fair, the children's need for safety, for belonging and for success may be met. In addition, once a sense of safety and belonging is established, children are more likely to feel comfortable enough to represent their needs and views. Hence, exceptional and super-sensitive efforts will need to be made to help refugee children almost simultaneously build this sense of belonging and represent their experiences and needs.

McIntyre and Abrams (2021) rationalised that the paths refugee children pursued in an attempt to achieve a sense of home were affected by how accepted or rejected they felt in their new environment and how warmly their own contributions were received. This means that achieving success and a longer-term positive adaptation are constrained by the extent to which these youngsters are allowed to participate equally, as well as the degree to which they develop free and equal relationships with their new environments.

For Kohli (2011, pp. 314, 316), safety starts with seeking to gain the legal right to settle in the host country, such as securing 'Leave to Remain' status in England or while they are awaiting the outcome of their application. However, Syrian refugee children in Lebanon rarely gain this legal right, even in the long term. Therefore, for them, establishing safety means obtaining sanctuary when they reach a non-conflict-affected host country, even when this sanctuary is not a legal right. Being and feeling safe are closely related to being able to remain, albeit temporarily in the case of Syrian refugees in Lebanon.

We argue, therefore, that restoring some form of ordinary life – even in makeshift shelters – requires finding safety beyond the legal definitions. Safety may be found, instead, in day-to-day interactions, where the child experiences sustainable living patterns that promise stability such as being in a place of learning, having a circle of loving, compassionate and trustworthy parents, other adults and peers, and enjoying healthy enough conditions in which to live and prosper (see Figure 2.3).

Figure 2.3   'My precious family' by a Syrian refugee pupil at a MAPs education centre. © The authors.

Once this sense of home and belonging is established, such children are more likely to feel a stronger sense of entitlement to represent their views to others and participate in socio-political life (see Figure 2.4).

Exploring children's own representations

Many studies focus on policy relating to displaced children (Sidhu & Taylor, 2007; Keddie, 2012; McIntyre & Hall, 2018; Karam, Monaghan & Yoder, 2016) but few focus on social injustices within the children's experiences of learning, teaching and school (see Osler, 2016). As with much educational research, little attention has been given to the feelings and thoughts of this young age-group of children and to those of refugees more broadly (Pinson & Arnot, 2007). To attend to these aspects of the displacement process, in this book, as well as employing Fraser's conceptualisation of social justice, we interrogate the children's words through the lens of Kohli's (2011) aforementioned theory about the three fundamental needs of refugee and asylum-seeking children. We believe these needs are more likely to be fulfilled when justice is maximised across Fraser's three dimensions of social justice.

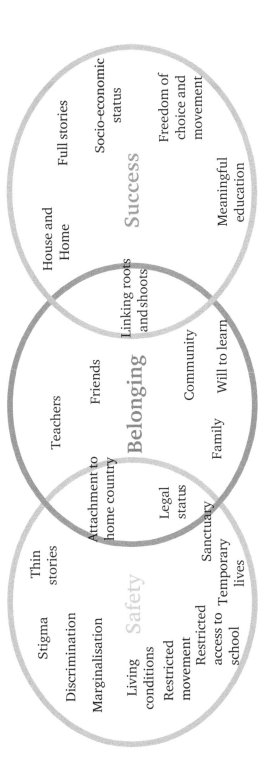

Figure 2.4 Kohli's main processes of resettlement after forced displacement. Source: Adapted from Kohli (2011).

Pinson and Arnot (2007, p. 406) referred to the gaps between 'on the one hand, disengagement of the central state, and, on the other, acts of compassion and recognition by teachers and schools'. These two specific aspects of social injustices among displaced children are addressed by Fraser's and Kohli's respective theories. When neither of these aspects is sufficiently addressed, this can be seen as 'misrepresenting and/or rendering voiceless this group of children thus compromising parity of participation on this dimension of justice' (Keddie, 2012, p. 199). Novelli et al. (2019) emphasised that injustice could fuel the grievances that drove conflicts when explaining the significance of the fourth R, reconciliation. They argued, therefore, that addressing inequalities, including within schooling, was necessary 'to bring about sustainable peace and overcome the legacies of conflict' (p. 71).

In our next chapters (especially Chapter 4), we explore Fraser's normative conceptualisation of social justice as parity-of-participation in the temporary settlement of children in 'education centres' in Lebanon. There, they never achieve the legal right to remain or progress within the national education system but nonetheless establish a sense of safety through a feeling of belonging. We explore how this sense of safety – this revised notion of safety as stability within supportive networks, rather than legal safety – had implications for their willingness to represent themselves to their teachers and our research team. We also examine which particular ideas they felt the need to represent.

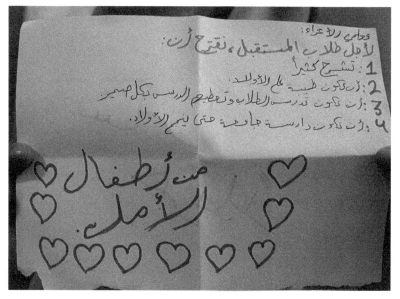

Figure 3.1   A MAPs pupil's letter to their teacher. © The authors.

My dear teachers

For the future students, we suggest that:
1- You explain thoroughly
2- To be kind to all children
3- To teach the students and convey the lessons honestly and fairly
4- The teacher should be a university graduate so children succeed.

Child of Hope from MAPs

3
Primary schooling and the UN's Sustainable Development Goals

Primary schooling is the period of education covering children's early years of formal learning. A series of reforms – starting with Education for All (EFA), which was propelled by the 1990 EFA World Conference in Jomtien, Thailand – have led governments and organisations to recognise the significance of primary education, not only as the right of every child to education provision but also as a critical component in healthy human development and, consequently, pathways to social justice. In this chapter, we describe the significance of primary education, particularly to vulnerable children and, even more specifically, to those internally or externally forcibly displaced due to armed conflict. We start by presenting the legal status of primary education according to international and national frameworks. We then highlight how primary education can provide the kind of support for lifelong healthy social and cognitive functioning that also addresses some of the social injustices exacerbated by illiteracy. We conclude by describing how primary education can be prioritised but also reduced through international targets for education and sustainable global development.

Legal status of primary education

Primary education holds a high-stakes position within international and national government legal frameworks. Article 28 of the UNCRC (United Nations, 1989) calls for countries that have ratified the Convention to 'make primary education compulsory and available free to all'. Of the 193 countries recognised by the UN, all but the United States (US) have ratified the UNCRC, a legally-binding instrument.[1] As defined under the UN International Standard Classification of Education (ISCED), primary education is the second of four levels of pre-tertiary education: pre-primary (or early childhood); primary; lower secondary; and secondary.[2] According to the ISCED, basic education comprises two stages: primary and lower secondary. A more detailed understanding of primary education is outlined in the glossary published by the Inter-agency Network for Education in Emergencies (INEE, 2022):

> Primary education provides learning and educational activities typically designed to provide students with fundamental skills in reading, writing, and mathematics, i.e. literacy and numeracy, and to establish a sound foundation for learning and solid understanding of core areas of knowledge and personal development, preparing for lower secondary education. It aims at learning at a basic level of complexity with little if any specialization.

These frameworks neither define a primary-school age range nor set primary education year levels. Nor do they state measurable indications of expectations by the end of primary education. Specific age groups or grade levels of primary education are left to governments to define. According to governments around the world, either 'primary' or 'elementary' is used when referring to this period of schooling before the secondary levels.

Most countries have structured their primary education levels as the first six years of schooling, and some have split the six years into two stages. All governments have a set age bracket for each grade level. In England, for example, primary schooling comprises two Key Stages, the first lasting two years and beginning at age four, the second lasting four years. Most countries have set 6 years of age as the required age to start school, while others, such as Finland and Rwanda, require children to start aged 7. When structuring primary education, Lebanon and Rwanda split the six years into two even cycles, three years each. The third cycle in Lebanon (years 7–9) is 'intermediate', followed by 'secondary' as the fourth cycle (years 10–12). Other countries, such as Cyprus, Spain, Latvia, Nigeria, Jordan and Egypt, treat the six years of primary schooling as a single block. A few countries, Brazil included, allocate the first nine years to primary education, while, in others, this stage covers either the first five years (India, France and Vietnam, for instance) or the first four years (Turkey, Syria and Lithuania, among others).

To ensure that education is available to, and attended by, all children, governments around the world have put laws in place to ensure

Table 3.1 Number of years of free, compulsory schooling legislated by governments

Years	No of countries	Examples
5	3	Myanmar, Togo, Vietnam
6	12	Cameroon, Haiti, Liberia
7	5	Lesotho, Namibia, Zambia
8	12	Croatia, India, Italy, South Sudan
9	21	Bosnia & Herzegovina, China, Iran, Japan, Nigeria, Lebanon, Rwanda, Switzerland, Yemen
10	11	Chad, Denmark, Nepal, Norway, Spain
11	23	Colombia, Kazakhstan, Malaysia, Russian Federation, Sudan, Venezuela
12	79	Afghanistan, Brazil, Canada, Cuba, Egypt, Finland, Iraq, Jordan, Pakistan, Palestine, Sweden
13	19	Australia, Congo, Germany, New Zealand, Sri Lanka, United Kingdom

Source: Based on data from the UNESCO Institute for Statistics (2019)

that education is both free and compulsory. The number of years of free and compulsory education, however, varies from one country to another, ranging from 5 to 13 years. Drawing on datasets from the UNESCO Education Profiles (UNESCO Institute for Statistics, 2019), Table 3.1 lists the number of countries that have determined a given number of free and compulsory years' schooling as protected by law. A majority of countries refer to the allocated years of free and compulsory education as 'basic education', which comprises the first nine years of schooling; with some such as Colombia, Switzerland and Brazil including pre-school. Despite the legal commitment to provide free education, state schools in some countries (Lebanon, Australia, New Zealand, Sudan and Egypt, among others) ask for fees that are invoiced as stationery supplies, exams or service charges.

Headteachers (principals) in Lebanon explained during informal conversations with one of us how the fee arrangements work. State schools in Lebanon charge parents of children in Grades 1–9 a nominal fee, which can range from 25,000 LBP to 120,000 LBP (in a rural school in North Lebanon, for instance) and up to 240,000 LBP (in Beirut). This covers costs such as diesel for heating in the winter, kindergarten activities, and paper and ink for photocopy machines.[3] A principal in North Lebanon reported during an informal conversation that large families in rural areas found this quite costly and, thus, had to turn to the local municipality for support. Since the influx of Syrian refugees into Lebanon after 2012, however, international donor agencies continue to cover all state school fees for host community children in Grades 1–9 and all Syrian refugee children (those who were able to access the provision) in second-shift schools.

Secondary state education in Lebanon is not free; parents pay a standard annual fee of 271,000 LBP. Following the country's economic collapse that devalued the LBP by over 90 per cent during 2020 and 2021, state schools have become more affordable. However, their purchasing power to secure basic resources such as stationery, fuel for heating and electricity has diminished to a point where the Lebanese Ministry of Education and Higher Education (MEHE) has turned to donor agencies to further support operational costs. These costs include payments to teachers to support their escalating transport costs and compensate for the salary shortfall caused by their devalued currency.

The legal frameworks that guarantee compulsory and free education do not guarantee access for all children. Nor do they guarantee completion of compulsory education or quality learning experiences. Children who have been forcibly displaced by war and taken refuge in a low- to middle-income country (LMIC) struggle to find places in host-nations' education systems. Refugees in host nation-states that are already plagued with the consequences of limited resources, corruption and/or post-armed-conflict social reconstruction initiatives themselves – such as Lebanon – are likely to face structural and socio-cultural barriers to state education (Dryden-Peterson et al., 2019). Such challenges and violations of children's right to education affect the vast majority of forcibly displaced people around the world. According to the United Nations High Commissioner for Refugees (UNHCR, 2020a), 85 per cent of the world's forcibly displaced have taken refuge in a low-income country, with only 17 per cent in high-income countries where educational resources are more accessible. Lebanon, for example, hosts 1.5 million Syrian refugees, the largest proportion of refugees in the world in relation to national population size (UNHCR, 2019b).[4] Although there were nearly 700,000 Syrian children of school age registered as being in Lebanon in the school year 2018–19, 58 per cent of them were out of school (UNHCR, 2019c). Many children in low-income countries who do access primary education struggle to stay on at school following this stage. From 2010 to 2015, only 83 per cent of children around the world completed six years of primary schooling (UNESCO, 2017/18); and, based on limited country-specific data after 2015, we see primary education completion rates at only 54 per cent in Iraq, 28 per cent in Pakistan and 24 per cent in Nigeria (UNESCO Institute for Statistics, 2019).

Quality primary education for child development and social justice

The emphasis on quality in primary education discourse is a reminder that the provision of schooling, as noted in the seminal work of Bush and Saltarelli (2000), can do as much harm as good; for example, where children suffer disrespectful treatment, this, too, may lead to a lack of learning. Moreover, support for child learning and other areas of development requires more than just the availability of education or access to it. While underlining the significance of primary education to children who are made vulnerable through forced migration and displacement, we outline next some key indicators of the kind of education we consider most appropriate to supporting the learning of forcibly displaced children and achieving social justice for them.

Primary education for child development

Primary education provision can be critical for optimal support of children's cognitive, physical, socio-emotional and linguistic development. Neuroscientific research on child development shows that the nature of children's relationships with other children and adults, exposure to different forms of stress, and responses to changing situations in childhood shape the brain architecture that largely determines how they continue to function throughout adulthood. In the child's early years, their stable relationships and reciprocated interactions with adults enable them to build healthy relationships later on (National Scientific Council on the Developing Child, 2004). Early childhood experiences also determine the neural wiring for key executive functions such as memory, emotional self-regulation and inhibitory controls (Center on the Developing Child, 2011).

The construction of neural architecture is most vulnerable during the earliest years of a child's life. Chronic exposure to neglect and violence – such as those associated with forced displacement, armed conflict or domestic violence – generates toxic stress. Under such stress, children's brains reshape into survival mode, reducing the usage and, consequently, the development of areas such as the prefrontal cortex, responsible for higher-level thinking and language learning (Shonkoff et al., 2012). Despite the unique ability of the brain to re-form neural connections throughout the lifespan, its developmental plasticity (or capacity to actually change or restructure) lessens as we age (National Scientific Council on the Developing Child, 2007). Moreover, the critical period for forming synapses for higher cognitive functions peaks during the first two years of life and begins to gradually decline throughout primary and secondary school years. Hence, primary education is critical for those developmental areas that have been hindered by adversity during children's most sensitive periods of growth in the early years but are still capable of establishing foundations for lifelong learning, resilience and emotional self-regulation.

Championing social justice through primary education

Ensuring that *all* children complete quality primary education addresses many of the social injustices associated with marginalised children who are rendered vulnerable, especially by violence and neglect. For children affected by forced displacement in particular, we identify at least two elements of child development that primary education needs to support for parity-of-participation. Primary schooling must ensure that all children (1) acquire a minimum command of literacy and numeracy and (2) receive the psychosocial and emotional support or even rehabilitation they might need.

A basic command of literacy and numeracy and a healthy state of socio-emotional wellbeing are requisite to equitable participation across the various spheres of everyday life, including the labour market, environmental sustainability, political participation and appropriate social interactions. These two elements facilitate children's confidence and ability to participate in forming healthy relationships, learning alongside peers and addressing political or environmental struggles at home. Improving the quality of primary and pre-primary education has, indeed, made opportunities for participation more equitable for children in low-income families in many countries and contexts. Hart and Risley (1992; 1995) showed that early-years children who are living in poverty or from low-income families are less likely to interact in family conversations than those from middle-income families. Importantly, these authors also found that the more limited nature of the verbal interactions they observed within lower-income-family talk prohibits the beneficial extended activities that are more possible in higher-income families, who tend to converse more. For example, they are less likely to read their children stories or take them to see performing arts. Consequently, children in lower-income families demonstrate more limited growth in their vocabulary over time (Hart & Risley, 1995) and exhibit a larger gap in IQ measures when compared with their peers from higher-income families (Hart & Risley, 1992).

By completing primary education, children are more likely to have gained basic literacy or received the necessary support to acquire the competencies needed to demonstrate a functional command of numbers. Children who acquire a minimum command of literacy and numeracy, for example, find it easier to participate in managing everyday affairs. A longitudinal study in Indonesia (classified as one of the low- and middle-income countries) found that interventions supporting pre-primary education (such as raising public awareness, building early-years learning centres, facilitating teacher training, organising playgroups and so on) had narrowed the school achievement gap between children from lower- and higher-income families (Jung & Hasan, 2016). These interventions not only raised the profile of pre-primary education but also ensured that children at the pre-school level could participate in transformative and sustainable community projects.

Children affected by toxic stress and chronic exposure to violence, neglect and struggles for survival – under circumstances such as child labour and early marriage – will most likely struggle to use higher-level thinking and are more likely to engage in antisocial behaviour and discontinue school (Shonkoff et al., 2012). Hence, the provision of support to help recover from, or manage, such trauma is essential in any education programme for refugee children. For Syrian refugee children in Lebanon, for example, policymakers and education programme developers from local and international NGOs have developed 'psycho-social support (PSS)' (MEHE, 2016) and 'social and emotional learning (SEL)' (Aziz et al., 2020) for formal education and NFE. However, robust evidence of how PSS and SEL are facilitated in education programmes for Syrian refugee children in Lebanon is quite scarce – and sound evidence of their effectiveness even rarer.

What we do find, however, is that Syrian refugee and host-community children exposed to toxic stress may require an intervention designed to rehabilitate. Rehabilitation after conflict-related damage is a fundamental expression of social justice for it helps address damage that would hinder or prevent children's opportunities and right to participate. Akar (2019) noted that 'rehabilitation' could be a fifth 'R' in the '4 Rs' framework that Novelli et al. (2015) developed from Fraser's '3 Rs' of redistribution, recognition and representation as social justice. For example, rehabilitation through education programmes has been pivotal for child soldiers in Sierra Leone returning to participation in learning and ordinary society (Betancourt et al., 2008). Similar principles apply to the mental health of children affected by conflict, such as Syrian refugee children who have lost a home, a parent or a friend or relative; witnessed destruction caused by warfare; or live in a home environment characterised by violence and neglect. Rehabilitation efforts, such as the case of children who suffered physical and emotional abuse in Romanian orphanages, can include input from a team of social workers, a training programme for parents, and financial subsidies (Nelson et al., 2013).

Studies on education and rehabilitation interventions for children suffering trauma demonstrate that not all primary education provision will support vulnerable children's development and address social injustices. Children with conflict-related trauma require a primary education, facilitated by qualified professionals, that is accompanied by a continuous rehabilitation programme for their transition into any future education curriculum that requires the high-level cognitive functions essential for learning a second language, critical thinking and problem-solving. There is also the need for meaningful work with parents to build up the healthiest approaches to learning and teaching. Of course, there is no homogenous trauma profile, and even the most well-meaning programmes can be misaligned with needs. Primary schooling for vulnerable children can provide them with the experiences necessary to recover, survive and flourish by returning to healthy participation in social activities; or it can actually exacerbate the stress and harmful impact of neglect and direct violence. We recognise that communities living under crises require specific contextualisation of their education, psychosocial support and rehabilitation programmes. These would support not only particular learning needs but also children's capacity to function and contribute within their communities and broader society.

International instruments and targets for free, compulsory primary schooling

Ensuring that all children have opportunities to complete primary education has long been a priority across the international community. In 1966, the UN published the International Covenant on Economic, Social and Cultural Rights (ICESCR), which, as of 2023, has 171 states parties. Article 13 of the ICESCR called for primary education to be free and compulsory for all children and declared that states parties should proactively ensure that children do, indeed, complete their primary schooling. More than two decades later, primary schooling provision became international law through the 1989 UNCRC, which required its 196 states parties to ensure provision of free and compulsory primary education for all children. Subsequently, international frameworks reinforced the right to education as a global priority through international targets and standards, some of which are described next.

In 1990, EFA gained strong momentum as a global movement through the aforementioned World Conference, 'Meeting Basic Learning Needs', hosted in Jomtien. One outcome of the Conference was the 'World Declaration on Education for All'. Under the fifth of its ten articles, primary education was proclaimed as the 'main delivery system for the basic education of children outside the family'. It maintained that primary education 'must be universal, ensure that the basic learning needs of all children are satisfied, and take into account the culture, needs, and opportunities of the community' (UNESCO, 1990, p. 6). The Declaration was appended by a framework for action that called for countries to set EFA targets according to their policy frameworks.

A decade later, in 2000, a further conference in Dakar, Senegal, revised the framework for action and produced 'The Dakar Framework for Action'. This reaffirmed that primary education 'should be free, compulsory and of good quality' (UNESCO, 2000, p. 12) as Goal 2 of its six goals. In its vision for Universal Primary Education, Goal 2 called for the removal of all possible costs that may be incurred by families, including transport, school meals, books and uniforms. Under this framework, governments were also expected to implement extra measures to ensure that children with special educational needs or disabilities or those from impoverished and remote communities attended and completed primary education. While the Dakar Framework attempted to define quality indicators for primary education, including that it should provide 'relevant content' (UNESCO, 2000, p. 16), it nevertheless placed greater emphasis on calling for proactive measures to attain universal enrolment and ensure that children completed their primary schooling.

During the same year as the Dakar conference, the UN hosted the Millennium Summit and, with the commitment of 189 UN member states, published the 'Millennium Development Goals' (MDGs). These eight goals were to have been achieved by 2015. Goal 2 was to 'Achieve universal primary education', supported by one target: 'Ensure that, by 2015, children everywhere, boys and girls alike, will be able to complete a full course of primary schooling'. The three progress indicators for this goal were: '(2.1) Net enrolment ratio in primary education;

(2.2) Proportion of pupils starting Grade 1 who reach last grade of primary; and (2.3) Literacy rate of 15–24 year-olds, women and men' (United Nations, 2003, p. 3). While these indicators clearly lacked narrative descriptions of possible approaches, foreseeable challenges and qualitative measures, MDG 2 maintained the vision that all children around the world would complete primary schooling.

The universal mission of primary education for all children was further reinforced and elaborated in Goal 4 of the 17 Sustainable Development Goals (SDGs) set by the UN for the period 2015–30. Goal 4 touches on several dimensions of primary education, including:

1. ensuring that all girls and boys complete primary education (target 4.1)
2. ensuring the provision of quality early childhood education to prepare children for primary education (target 4.2)
3. ensuring that primary school teachers have received the necessary training that qualifies them to teach (target 4.c).

The SDGs were received with critical reviews including, for example, the observation that they 'do not adequately address the effects of conflict, militarisation, labour migration, and war-driven displacement on development', particularly in the Arab region (El-Zein et al., 2016, p. 1). An attempt was made in 2019 to ensure that the SDGs made direct reference to refugees. However, while Nahmias and Baal (2019) reported that a new indicator was approved to be added (ostensibly, '16.3.3 Proportion of population who are refugees by country of origin'), the official SDG website still does not have any such indicator listed.[5]

Also, SDG 4 appears to take for granted that education is almost unconditionally a positive force. Van Ommering (2019) argues that this particular goal overlooked the harms that education can inflict on children, particularly those vulnerable to crises, through its target of absolute access to education (such as permitting *any* education context) and also through the Framework for Action. The latter views education as 'fundamentally protective for children … [as it] provides them with tools to rebuild their lives and communities' (UNESCO et al., 2015, p. 27). Hence, SDG 4 presupposes that all education provision is safe and nurturing – an assumption that Harber (2004) and Bush and Saltarelli (2000) have shown is not always the case.

Furthermore, the targets are limited to changes in numbers or ratios. For example, one progress indicator relating to children completing primary education is an increase in the number of children enrolled or who have completed primary education. In a similar vein, with regard to teachers being suitably qualified to teach, successful attainment of the target is evaluated in terms of an increase in the number of teachers with recognised formal qualifications. This emphasis on quantitative measures, rather than explorations of actual quality, distracts educationists from advancing discourses on learning and developing approaches to engaging children in collaborative, dialogic and critical pedagogies and any consideration of rehabilitation, special educational needs and disabilities (see also Chapter 8).

Schooling provision for Syrian refugee children

Lebanon's MEHE has made attempts to meet the education needs of Syrian refugee children, primarily by adding the aforementioned 'second-shifts' to the timetable in a number of state primary schools. This second-shift provision is specifically designed to enable Syrian refugee children to attend at least a few lessons for a reduced number of hours in the afternoons, taught by Lebanese staff (UNHCR, 2016b), rather than having no access to schooling at all.

According to the MEHE-published lists of those state schools assigned the task of providing second-shift schooling, there were: 259 schools for the academic year 2015–16; 348 schools for 2018–19 (the academic year in which our main research project for this book was undertaken); and 360 schools for 2019–20. Although the number of state schools introducing second-shift provision slowly increased year on year, there remained, at the time of writing, a large shortfall in the number of places available. Of the estimated 666,491 school-age Syrian refugee children in Lebanon in 2018, a third were enrolled in the second-shift state schools, and just over a third of those of compulsory school age (6–14 years) were not in any form of learning (UNICEF et al., 2019).

Despite this notional provision (which, under the international gaze, appears helpful), Syrian refugee children in Lebanon still face considerable barriers to learning. The country's initial response to securing education for these children focused largely on physical enrolment, while it overlooked sustainable mechanisms to provide social and emotional support and engage parents as critical actors in facilitating the children's attendance and learning (Akar & Van Ommering, 2018). The language of instruction remains a barrier for Syrian children in these schools. All pupils in state schools, regardless of nationality, are required to follow the Lebanese curriculum, which is taught in a combination of Arabic, French and English (MEHE, 1997). In Syria, however, Arabic was the language used in schools when the refugee children were still there (which a few had attended prior to 2011). French was not widely taught until more advanced school grades. And the children's familiarity with English was limited: indeed, there was no generational expectation of the need for English and, therefore, most parents lacked sufficient knowledge of English to support (or, in many cases, see the value of) their children studying it as a second language (Human Rights Watch, 2016; Immerstein & Al-Shaikhly, 2016). The Arabic language competence of the Syrian children is comparatively high but does not serve them well in a system dominated by French or English.

In addition to these linguistic barriers to learning, alongside ease of transport, safety concerns and other issues, another significant factor reported to be detrimental to the children's engagement with learning is an economic one (UNICEF, 2016a; UNHCR & REACH, 2014): the cost to families of providing books, supplies, uniforms and, anecdotally, other 'fees' charged at school level, even though schooling is notionally free of charge (Shuayb et al., 2020). Additionally, it has long been the perception of Syrian families that, even if they were able to source funding to enable their children to attend state schools, the latter would encounter hostility in these institutions. Indeed, many *have* faced bullying and corporal punishment as they were singled-out for being Syrian (Human Rights Watch, 2016). One study found that 'the majority of Syrian students enrolled in Lebanese public [i.e. state] schools reported regular physical and verbal abuse from the teaching staff and principals, as well as bullying from their Lebanese peers' (Shuayb et al., 2014, p. 10).

Moreover, much research suggests that, as schools may, in some cases, have been 'forced' to implement second-shifts, these were not always enthusiastically or effectively run. Consistent with trends identified in Kingdon et al. (2014, p. 3), practices in the second-shift were 'at best neutralising and at worst undermining' the initiative. This contributed to the high reported early-dropout rates of Syrian children from Lebanese state schools – twice the Lebanese national average (UNICEF & Save the Children, 2012, p. 5).

Many refugee children were unable (for largely financial reasons) or unwilling (due to safety concerns or not seeing an applicable purpose in the labour market) to exercise their rights to and within education. This is evidenced in the 'alarming and growing' rate of early marriage in girls (UNICEF, 2016a, p. 67) and in the child labour data (UNICEF, 2016a).

These indicators provide a vivid illustration of how education is being foregone in favour of essential survival activities (Jones & Ksaifi, 2016) arising from the scaling-down of World Food Programme support and parents being unable to secure income through legal, financially worthwhile and safe means (UNICEF, 2016b). Added to these problems that render schooling less accessible for Syrian refugee children, the Lebanese Government does not permit Syrian teachers to be employed, hence they are not in a position to ameliorate the huge demands consistently placed on teacher recruitment. Had they been allowed, they could have provided a context of continuity and shared culture for Syrian children, in keeping with the ideals of the INEE Minimum Standards and the general principles of the UNHCR strategy. This situation had not changed at the time of research in 2019 or, indeed, at the time of writing in 2023.

Severe economic pressures have meant that refugee families have, in many cases, remained in improvised tented communities in the cheapest and, often, least accessible parts of Lebanon (see Figure 3.2). These are areas where the poorest sections of the host community were already located and where public services such as education were already particularly stretched and of poor quality (Jones & Ksaifi, 2016; UNICEF, 2015).

Figure 3.2 'From Syria to Lebanon' by a Syrian refugee pupil at a MAPs education centre. © The authors.

There have been some private educational facilities provided by the refugee community (paid and free). Among private schools, pupils generally followed the Lebanese Curriculum, but a small number followed the curriculum of the Syrian Coalition opposition government (with examination accreditation largely in Turkey) or the Syrian Curriculum, with children returning to Syria to take exams there (Shuayb et al., 2014).

Despite the Lebanese Government initially working with international actors in line with MEHE's strategic plan of implementing the Reaching All Children with Education (RACE) programme (MEHE, 2014) and its successor RACE II (MEHE, 2016), the high-level coordination that might have helped mitigate some of the barrier issues through the work of smaller NGOs was actually reduced in subsequent years. For instance, the government disbanded the UNHCR Education Sector Working Group in September 2014 (Buckner & Spencer, 2016). At the same time, donor funding (which is granted by international aid agencies) has not kept pace with the increasing demands made of the public sector (Culbertson & Louay, 2015). Education financing has been consistently below the amounts sought – for example, out of $366 million required in 2018, only $273 million was received (UNHCR, 2019a). These trends suggest that the humanitarian aid efforts managed via national and international governance can be said to be falling short of meeting the needs of refugee children in Lebanon. Consequently, with the state and trans-state sectors either unable or unwilling (or perhaps both) to meet the considerable funding requirements, a range of other actors have emerged to attempt to fill the gap with a variety of initiatives and programmes.

Education provision in Lebanon for the incoming Syrian children can be grouped into two main forms:

1. *Formal education* – schooling following a state-recognised curriculum, which may be delivered by public-sector or private operators
2. *NFE* – schooling with looser associations with the state's recognised curriculum and often a less formal practical set-up. Teaching is delivered by groups that are not usually recognised as part of an official educational system (Brock, 2011).

Such NFE programmes can range from unstructured learning in improvised classrooms to full-time provision closely mirroring a formal school model and can be run by a range of actors including national and international NGOs as well as members of the host and refugee communities themselves (Human Rights Watch, 2016; Shuayb et al., 2014). The provision delivered within NFE could entail, for instance, programmes involving community-based, full-time schooling that is not run by the state, does not fully deliver the approved Lebanese curriculum, and has no externally-accredited recognition of the learning achievements of the children (Shuayb et al., 2014). Case Study 1 focuses on precisely this kind of provision.

Taking into account public-sector provision as well as private providers and non-formal forms of schooling, at the time of our main research study and despite some increase in access, 54 per cent of school-age (3–18 years) Syrian children were classed as 'out of school' (UNHCR, 2019b). For children in the upper-secondary age range, even though they reported that they placed great value on education and would welcome meaningful opportunities to return to learning, only a meagre 6 per cent were actually engaged in any form of provision through secondary or technical/vocational schools (UNICEF et al., 2014; UNHCR, 2019b).

There was (and remains), therefore, a clear and ongoing crisis in education provision for children fleeing the Syrian conflict and taking refuge within the territory of Lebanon. As noted earlier, the Government of Lebanon has, with the support of international agencies and donors, taken some steps to provide for the educational needs of these children. However, the provision that has been put in place has been predicated on the broad perception (which still pertains) among the Lebanese authorities that the Syrian refugee situation should not be prolonged (Culbertson & Louay, 2015).

The personal testimonials of Syrian refugee children living in Lebanon that are captured in Chapter 4 provide a narrative description of certain dimensions of a quality primary education. These children were among a minority population of refugee children in Lebanon who had privileged (in relative terms) access to an education programme where teachers embraced and facilitated their participation. The children felt safe enough to tell of their experiences and their visions for a better education within their context of vulnerability, margin- alisation and forced displacement. Furthermore, the two case studies in Chapters 5 and 6 illustrate two very different contexts in which displaced Syrian refugees faced more of a struggle to secure safety and the sense of belonging necessary to thrive and flourish as empowered individuals.

Notes

1 For updates on ratification status, visit https://indicators.ohchr.org.
2 The ISCED can be consulted here: https://uis.unesco.org/en/topic/international-standard-classification-education-isced.
3 Prior to the economic collapse of November 2019, the currency was valued at 1,500 LBP to one US dollar. The collapse devalued the LBP by 90 per cent. In April 2023, the black market was selling one US dollar for 100,000 LBP.
4 A later UNHCR publication (2020b) notes the Government of Lebanon's estimate of 1.5 million Syrian refugees being hosted, although, of this number, only 918,874 were registered with UNHCR.
5 The indicator proposal and its metadata template can be accessed here: https://unstats.un.org/sdgs/files/iaeg-sdg/16.3%20Additional%20Indicator.zip. The official SDG definition for Goal 16 can be consulted here: https://sdgs.un.org/goals/goal16#targets_and_indicators.

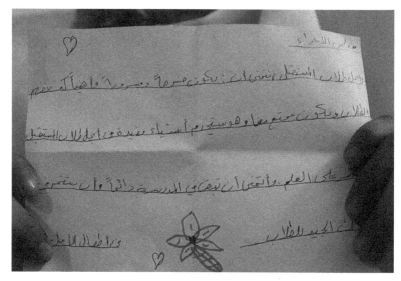

Figure 4.1 A MAPs pupil's letter to their teacher. © The authors.

My dear teachers

For the future students, we wish that: you'd be happy and content and also explain lessons well to students and be fun and use useful resources for the future students to be able to continue learning. I hope you'd stay and always teach at the school and continue with your good teaching of the students.

Child of Hope from MAPs

It's too late for me now, everything is lost. But my children still have a chance.

Parent, Beqaa Valley, Lebanon

4
Vulnerable displaced Syrian children's representations: Case study 1

Introduction

This chapter comprises two parts. Part 1 sets out in more detail the educational context of the children who participated in the research workshops of Case Study 1. It explores the broader landscape of education provision for Syrian refugees within Lebanon, where those specific children were residing at the time of field research (see Figure 4.2). In this first part, we also incorporate insights and reflections on the context shared by members of staff of MAPs, the organisation running the schools from which the children participating in the workshops were drawn, and some of the parents of children at the schools. These were gained through a series of semi-structured interviews with 16 parents, teachers and MAPs management staff in Lebanon. In Part 2 of this chapter, we narrate the children's own representations gathered through the research workshops. For those who wish to replicate or build on these activities, we first describe how we designed and facilitated the activities. The UCL Institute of Education reviewed and approved the ethical considerations for the data-gathering presented in both parts of this chapter.

MAPs – A non-formal school community serving Syrian refugees in Lebanon

Non-formal education at MAPs

Our research project was sited within the work of one NGO, MAPs – a Lebanon-registered organisation driven *by* members of the Syrian refugee community, *for* that community. They began their work in education in 2013 in response to the growing needs they saw around them within the Syrian refugee population. Their on-the-ground information and survey/scoping activity reports matched the contextual patterns outlined in Chapter 3. Hence, they resolved to concentrate their efforts in locations where they had identified the greatest need, in two broad areas within the Beqaa Valley: 1) in and around Arsal in the northeast and 2) the strip alongside the Damascus Highway between Saadnayel and the

Figure 4.2   Map of Syria and Lebanon. Source: Shutterstock.

Syrian border in the central part of the Valley. While various other NGOs are also involved in education in the area, including small initiatives led by Syrians within the refugee community, MAPs itself offers a unique range of services including humanitarian relief such as winterisation and clothing initiatives, vocational training, adult learning, higher education and healthcare. Its healthcare services include a number of free or low-cost clinics for both refugee and host communities, offering an extensive range of services such as breast cancer screening, dialysis and dental health as well as collaborative programmes in mental health care. Many of these initiatives are integrated into its work in education.

MAPs' main programme in education incorporates its management of nine 'teaching centres' (described variously as 'schools', 'learning centres' or 'teaching points') providing NFE. This encompasses teaching from early years (referred to locally as Community-Based Early Childhood Education) up to primary Grade 6 (at the time of research), as well as programmes in Basic Literacy and Numeracy for adolescents and young people. Of these, four centres are located in the region surrounding the town of Arsal and five in central Beqaa. Similar to some other NFE providers in the country, the MAPs centres therefore serve as a 'platform for greater education, protection, WASH (water, sanitation and hygiene) and food distribution provision for refugees' (Deane, 2016, p. 39).

Each of the nine MAPs centres was sited either within, or adjacent to, informal tented settlements. The locations were chosen by MAPs in response to the greatest numbers of children in those camps (or within easy walking distance); as well as with reference to the lack of available state schooling, the availability of land, and the willingness of local communities (and their leaders) to tolerate the establishment of such centres. The appearance of tented settlements near existing residential areas was sometimes perceived as a threat to security and wellbeing. Eliciting local views involved not only household surveys but also the rapid development of links with host communities and the building of trust with the Syrian families.

All of the centres within the organisation follow a broadly similar design: a collection of metal, static-caravan-style structures within a secure, fenced-off area, generally incorporating spaces cleared of rubbish and unused existing structures, which were repurposed as playgrounds (see Figure 4.3). In each of the centres, one of these caravans is dedicated to toilet and washing facilities, with clean, potable water freely available to all.

There is limited natural lighting in these caravans and they are vulnerable to extreme changes in temperature. In the winter, when

Figure 4.3 Typical example of a MAPs teaching centre, Beqaa, Lebanon.
Photo © Brian Lally.

temperatures can drop substantially below freezing, there is only
rudimentary heating at the front of each van in the form of diesel-
burning appliances, which is of course contingent on securing funds
for fuel. In the hotter months, when temperatures can rise above 40°C,
ventilation is supported by a simple fan, although the supply of mains
electricity is sporadic in many cases. Each teaching space accommodates
at least 30 pupils (the maximum number observed was 35) seated on
wooden benches, usually three per bench (see Figure 4.4).

The same physical spaces are generally provided for all learners,
regardless of age. However, two of the centres were later equipped with
a larger, square wooden hut structure that was used for the youngest
children. Due to the large demand for places, the schools operate
a double-shift model, usually with younger children attending from
8–12 pm each day, and then older learners coming from 12–4 pm. This
means that each space can service the needs of children between 4 and
15 years old. Many of the children are older than they would ordinarily
be for each school grade, due to missing entire years of schooling because
of their displacement.

While these physical conditions provide less-than-ideal teaching
spaces for child-driven, collaborative and dialogic pedagogies, they were
a practical and pragmatic solution to urgent needs. Their temporary
nature meant that they were not only cheaper to establish but also

Figure 4.4   Typical example of the interior of a MAPs teaching caravan, Beqaa, Lebanon. Photo © Brian Lally.

more readily accepted by local host communities. They were, and remain, visibly temporary structures, and thus compliant with local legal requirements. This also gave the organisation built-in flexibility. When, on occasion, whole communities in camps are further displaced, the learning centres are able to move with the families they serve.

There was also an added symbolism to the impermanence of the mobile classrooms. In the early years of the Syrian conflict in particular, their deployment supported the optimistic notion within the Syrian community that the dangers would abate and that returning home within a limited timeframe would be feasible (as reflected in many of the children's words captured later in this chapter). The acquisition of the mobile classrooms formed part of an external recognition of the damage that had been done to the physical infrastructures underpinning education in Syria. The putative thinking was that, upon the return of the refugees to their homeland, the classrooms could be quickly and cheaply relocated to Syrian sites where schools had been destroyed or were not immediately usable, thereby minimising further disruption to children's learning.

The very location of the schools also holds symbolic as well as pragmatic value. Beyond easing families' fears of the dangers around transport (and the often very significant costs of that, relative to their means), the fact that the schools are physically right at the heart of the communities they serve, established from within the Syrian refugee population, serves as a powerful totem of agency and hope. It also helps reframe the community as more than passive recipients of humanitarian aid: 'We are not just sitting around waiting, with our hands out', as Dr Fadi Al-Halabi, the founder and General Director of MAPs, put it.

The safe, secure play areas and use of the locations for community activities such as health-promotion initiatives or medical/dental campaigns only serve to reinforce this notion of the community itself identifying and seeking to meet its own needs. This was also referred to by the children themselves, as their testimonies later in this chapter show. Further, the fact that these activities are organised with a particular emphasis on the younger members of that community shifts the focus beyond the immediate challenges and struggles of daily life as a refugee in Lebanon, toward longer-term thinking. As one parent reflected: 'If we are talking about education, we are talking about our children and their futures and that has to be a hopeful thing'. The sense of regularity and stability facilitated through the centres thereby helps to foster exactly the revised notion of 'safety' outlined in our theoretical conceptualisation in Chapter 2. Even within the permanent temporality of the informal context of both school and camp, conditions can be nurtured in which children can potentially develop a powerful sense of belonging and community.

Across all nine learning centres, each operating two shifts per day, MAPs has been able to serve up to 3,000 children each year. This figure does fluctuate, driven by availability of finances rather than demand. The staff are overwhelmingly drawn from within the Syrian community, serving on a voluntary basis to stay in line with the legal employment restrictions on hiring Syrians without legal documentation for paid work in the sector. Funding for MAPs' education programme has come from a range of sources since its establishment in 2013. The bulk of the finance to cover initial set-up costs came from the wider Syrian and Arab diaspora, through a mixture of private sponsorship and donations from smaller NGOs, as well as funding of some aspects of the work by larger international organisations and embassies. Insecurity of funding year-to-year and general scarcity of funds are common features of education projects in humanitarian contexts, and Lebanon is no exception. Smaller organisations such as MAPs are often permanently under-funded, leading to challenges around the availability and quality of resources, as well as staff retention. Humanitarian funding for education in Lebanon, while never matching the needs, has actually declined since 2018 (Human Rights Watch, 2022).

Following the concept of building the learning centres and developing their work from within the community, MAPs recognised the skills capacity and potential among the Syrian refugees for delivering their own education provision. The displaced population, of course, includes the full range of professions and occupations needed to set up and run education institutions. They therefore sought out teachers, managers, caretakers and other staff, where possible, from within the community. Their services were supported by stipends to cover their expenses as volunteers – because (as mentioned earlier) in the legal landscape of Lebanon, Syrian refugees are not allowed to be employed or salaried in these fields of work (Errighi & Griesse, 2016). In Chapter 7, we explore the views of some of the staff about the nature of their work and what it means to them. From the outset, MAPs identified the need for ongoing professional development for its staff, especially the teachers. This was explicitly designed not only for initial teacher training but also to develop the skills and capacities of those who already had teaching experience. The curricula for teacher education programmes drew on the particular needs-profiles of displaced children and reflected the nature of the teaching spaces, as well as the chronic lack of resources and materials.

Perspectives of MAPs' staff

Curriculum decisions are also impacted by funding availability and not only by the reduced classroom hours available in school arising from the dual-shift model. For example, restricted funding resources in some years meant that some subjects were prioritised as core, leaving others such as sports or arts reduced or even removed. Likewise, limited budgets could not secure teachers or materials for non-core learning activities. Within these ongoing uncertainties, wherever possible, the organisation had initially put lessons in place based on the Syrian curriculum, thus replicating to a degree that formal system in a non-formal setting. This decision was rooted in the expectation that the Syrian refugee community would repatriate within a year or so. However, as the conflict became more protracted, it became clear that children would not be able to return soon to their homeland.

The MAPs management team then sought to curate a curriculum that would not only allow the children to learn and develop in ways that would 'help them to rebuild our country' (Syrian MAPs teacher) but also offer them the chance to integrate into the Lebanese system and

Figure 4.5 'Sad in Lebanon' by a Syrian refugee pupil at a MAPs education centre. © The authors.

thus progress their learning beyond Grade 6. As one centre manager explained: 'We had to admit to ourselves that we are going to be here for some time, perhaps many years, so we have to prepare the children for life here as well as when we go back'. Figure 4.5 depicts one student's illustration of sadness at their current living conditions, while Figure 4.6 shows the contrast perceived by another refugee child between their life in Syria and their life in Lebanon.

MAPs Director Dr Al-Halabi articulates the duality of this vision as: 'You have to work as though we will be here forever and, at the same time, as though we will go home to Syria tomorrow'. The model that has emerged in the MAPs programme, notwithstanding the afore-mentioned restrictions, broadly follows a condensed version of the Lebanese primary school curriculum, with lessons in Arabic Language, Mathematics, Science and English as its core. In addition, there is a

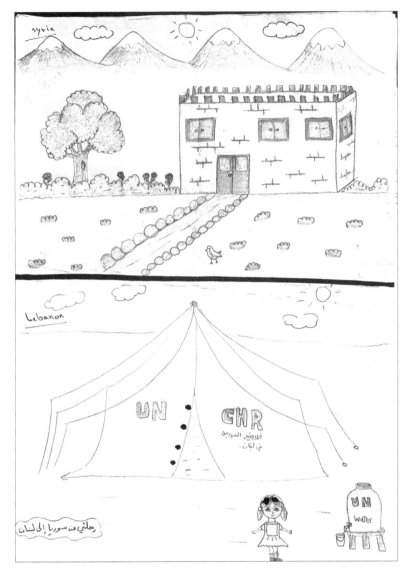

Figure 4.6 'My journey from Syria to Lebanon' by a Syrian refugee pupil at a MAPs education centre. © The authors.

more sporadic programme of 'Civics' as well as an infrequent schedule of 'Activities', which includes sports, art and drama when resources permit.

MAPs' leadership team has wanted to provide high-quality psycho-social support – in part, as they believe 'it will help the children to be ready to learn', as one teacher put it. One of the MAPs centre managers reported that they had trialled some programmes in the past but were concerned that the team members delivering this specialist work were neither officially trained nor certified. The concern here was that the interventions might have made things worse for the children, not better. More recently, MAPs has been working with a specialist psychologist to develop a tailored programme, contextualised for the children in its centres, to support the emotional literacy of the young people in its care (this was being piloted at the time of research). While that scheme was in preparation, they resolved to deliver more 'indirect' support through the provision of extra-curricular activities such as art, sports and structured play, partly as a way to work on social/emotional and behavioural skills such as teamwork and communication, and partly to meet the broader learning aims of these sessions. However, as previously noted, the scale of provision of these activities has been limited by the organisation's access to funding. The manager of one of the schools captured this dynamic succinctly: 'How can we prioritise sport over learning to read?'

One major function of MAPs' education programme has explicitly been to enable the children, who would otherwise not engage (or be able to engage) with other forms of education, to transition into the Lebanese formal system for Grade 7 onward, ideally leading toward secondary education. As the manager of one of the aforementioned learning centres confirmed, this constitutes a shift in philosophical outlook for an organisation that was initially envisaged as providing education only on a temporary basis:

> We thought we were setting up schools so that the children would at least have something to keep them going until we can go home. We thought it would take months, no more than a year.

Inevitably, this expectation had to be revised, and the manager explained MAPs' current perspective thus:

> Our main purpose is to fill the gap in MEHE provision due to lack of capacity and transport so that we get our children prepared for Grade 7; but we will take anyone, even if they don't want to carry on after Grade 6.

The overall curriculum thus appears to demonstrate some adaptability, in principle, in line with Tomaševski's rights-based approach (2001). However, it is far from clear that all teachers, parents and learners share this understanding of its adaptability, despite this being one of the core principles of the curriculum. For example, in focus group discussions, some parents expressed the view that their children would either continue their learning back in Syria or else be forced to enter the employment market in Lebanon after Grade 6. Indeed, some parents suggested that under no circumstances did they want their children to be educated within the Lebanese state system or by non-Syrian teachers. Another centre manager expressed frustration at the challenges – including issues around language of instruction – of attempted integration within, and transition to, the formal provision of the public sector. As noted earlier, the Lebanese system includes lessons in Science and Maths that are delivered in English and French. MAPs is aware of the importance of teaching English to the Syrian children – not least, to enable them to cope in these subject areas should they transfer to Lebanese schools. However, according to this same centre manager, 'the Lebanese kids are much more advanced in English than our kids; they have much more time in school – we don't have as many hours in school each day, and they [the Lebanese] start to learn English in KG [kindergarten or pre-school]'. Further, MAPs is only able to offer provision for eight months of the year, significantly fewer than its Lebanese counterparts. This inevitably impacts on the overall learning progression that the children are able to make – children who have in many cases already missed months or years of schooling.

Transition into Grade 7 and beyond may not, in and of itself, be a direct indicator of the relative quality of learning outcomes for the children, not least because of the very small numbers even seeking to transfer. Nonetheless, transition is one indicator that the organisation has set for itself and, of course, reflects the position of the schools in the broader educational landscape. At the time of our main research project for this book (2019), very few children were moving on from the MAPs schools into formal Lebanese provision for Grade 7 and beyond, the gateway to recognised qualifications. Progress has been made in this regard since then and, indeed, MAPs itself now offers some provision in Grades 7, 8 and 9. It has also developed partnerships with another NGO offering a model of private schooling (at no cost to families) for Grade 7 for some of the children leaving Grade 6, at two of its centres.

The reasons behind MAPs children's non-participation in education beyond Grade 6 are several and complex, and go beyond the critical barriers of availability and accessibility. While economic factors are frequently cited, the perception of many parents is also that their children would be subject to aggression and abuse from staff and children if they were to transfer into Grade 7 in Lebanese state schools. Our focus-group research with parents made it clear that they would strongly prefer their children to continue to learn within the Syrian-led informal provision, once again expressing a preference for Syrian teachers.

Among children from the NFE sector, a further major barrier to continuing in education beyond basic cycles/primary years is accreditation and certification. Normally, NFE programmes regulated by MEHE are provided by NGOs to give children from any background learning support to enable them to subsequently enter the age-level year in Lebanese formal schooling. Among such NFE provision is the Basic Literacy and Numeracy programme and the Accelerated Learning Programme (ALP). The ALP is designed to deliver a highly condensed curriculum to children missing significant amounts of schooling, thereby enabling them (in theory, at least) to enter state school. However, some NGOs (like MAPs) provide full-year ALPs, particularly for Syrian refugee children who are unable to enrol in (state school) second-shift provision. Typically, through public and licensed private Lebanese institutions, the MEHE issues credentials to confirm the completion of each school-year level. However, the MEHE has stopped short of providing credentials that would officially recognise NFE programmes providing grade-level education. NGOs including MAPs are therefore unable to access the system of official certification for children completing each academic year of learning; and this certification is required in order for children to be permitted access to the subsequent phase or even year of schooling in the national system. This means, in practice, that it is virtually impossible for these children to attend the next grade-level in formal state or private schools in Lebanon.

MAPs does, however, issue its own, internal certificates of completion and achievement each school year. This practice is based on a schedule of structured assessments throughout the school year, devised and delivered by its own staff. The model for these tests and exams is very closely rooted in the structures familiar to staff and parents from the Syrian system. While some staff express concern at the amount of curriculum time and focus that goes into such purely internal and non-standardised endeavours, the organisation's leadership is steadfast in its belief in the value of this work. In particular, one senior manager, while acknowledging the limitations of these tests, was very keen that they remain in place to signal to the families that the education centres 'are doing what proper schools do'. In other words, the internal certification is undertaken to convey a measure of quality and reassure the community of the validity of the work of the schools. This position resonated with the perception expressed by one parent, commenting on other non-formal provision that her children had previously attended, that 'all they did was sing, play and give the children toast, they didn't learn anything'.

While the lack of access to government accreditation for the work of the children is clearly a major problem for the organisation, it also presents some interesting possibilities. Not having to comply with the imposed restrictions of formalised curricular obligations affords an opportunity for meaningful adaptation to the unique needs of Syrian refugee children. This includes their needs as learners in very challenging, ongoing circumstances, and also what they might require as they enter the labour force, especially under the hostile and restrictive employment conditions of being a refugee in Lebanon. For example, such flexibility has enabled MAPs to develop and implement the aforementioned psychosocial support and cultural activities designed to preserve and foster Syrian identity as well as humanitarian values. Such an approach is entirely consistent with aspects of Fraser's (2008) conception of recognition, specifically in seeking to address the needs of the learners within the context of their lived reality.

MAPs has therefore adopted a utilitarian approach to education, including focusing on literacy and numeracy, with an emphasis throughout on achieving cognitive development, emotional literacy and learning stamina too. Its approach also seeks to provide education's associated protections against possible oppression, the threat of which lies around every corner for Syrian children, as well as broader psychosocial support. Critical thinking, innovation and problem-solving skills thus become not just 'nice to have' attributes but rather essential characteristics for children to master, to survive and thrive in this context. This accent on the nature, quality and purpose of education itself – as opposed to a narrower focus only on official certification – presents a critical shift in non-formal provision in conflict settings. It is noteworthy that this arises not out of what might be dismissed as an indulgent 'purity of education' approach but, rather, out of a practical, pragmatic, and more truly child-centred framing of education provision in the face of systemic and arguably deliberate restrictions on children's access to learning. A clear example of such thinking in practice is MAPs' Educate to Innovate project. This takes advantage of the less-than-ideal reduction in teaching hours arising from the dual-shift model and leverages MAPs' vocational training facilities from its other programmes. Since the older children are taught in the schools in the afternoon shifts, this also means that – unless they are working to earn money for the families (for example, picking vegetables) – they are available for classes in the mornings too.

Throughout the year, funding permitting, MAPs takes the older children to its vocational training centre one morning a week. Here they follow a carousel programme centred around courses in art, computing, applied science and robotics. These sessions are designed and delivered by volunteer staff from within the Syrian community who did not originally train as teachers. Rather, they are qualified and experienced professionals such as engineers, software designers and artists. There is no formal curriculum that needs to be followed. The schemes are devised and organically developed to serve the needs and interests of the children in each group. For example, one project hugely popular with the children involves them building small solar chargers, which they then take home to their parents to use in their tents to power mobile phones. Much use is made of recycled or salvaged materials, be it to teach the principles of hydraulics or computer design, learn about electrical circuits, or explore artistic possibilities. Arguably, this allocation of resources by the organisation, despite their limited nature, constitutes an efficient and positive redistribution and contributes, if only in a small way, to the young learners' ability to enjoy social justice through parity-of-participation (Fraser, 2008).

MAPs, then, uses the flexibility inherent to NFE and informal education to its advantage, developing and tailoring courses and activities to meet the needs of its own community. This is in line with the mode of 'continued recalibration in their approach to education programmes' (Shuayb et al., 2014, p. 12) that is associated with other informal/non-formal providers. Importantly, this approach sits alongside MAPs' commitment to more traditional elements of the curriculum, especially literacy and numeracy. Its teaching centres have become vital spaces of safety and learning as well as being visible focal points for highly marginalised people. In other words, its efforts are explicitly designed to foster a sense of safety and belonging within a context of high expectation–high support for the children to succeed in their academic pursuits, in consonance with Kohli's framework (2011).

The staffing and running of the provision *for* refugees and *by* refugees means that the community is endeavouring to meet the needs it is best placed to identify and resolve, meaning that the organisation promotes and embodies agency and dignity. Thus, it constitutes a direct expression of representation within a social justice framing (Fraser, 2008). The very limitations that the teachers experience due to their own refugee status, including the traumas and challenges they themselves face, also have the potential to be assets in that they can directly empathise with the children, given the right training and development. Similarly, the limitations on resources and the restrictions of the national education landscape can offer the potential to innovate. Our research project clearly demonstrated just how much both empathy and innovation are craved, appreciated and valued by the children, as illustrated in the next part of this chapter.

THE POTENTIAL FOR DISPLACED CHILDREN TO ENJOY REPRESENTATION OF THEIR OWN

> One child wrote:
>
> من علمني حرفا كنت له عبدا
>
> If someone teaches me even one letter, I will be in their debt for ever.

This second part of Chapter 4 focuses on the experiences and perspectives of the displaced Syrian children themselves, as expressed in their own words and images (see Figure 4.7, for example, for their idea of family as belonging). All of the children were living in the temporary settlements of Beqaa and Arsal in Lebanon, as explained earlier. This part explores the implications that their experiences of displacement may have, first, for their schooling and, second, for their participation in social interaction at local, national and global levels. We draw once again on Nancy Fraser's framework of social justice, in which parity-of-participation is equated with redistribution, recognition and representation, and on Ravi Kohli's framework of resettlement, which includes the need for safety, belonging and success. We investigate whether the current situation these children face is 'systematically depreciating some categories of people and the qualities associated with them', thereby constituting a gross miscarriage of justice (Fraser, 2018, p. 26). In particular, we focus on the potential for displaced children to enjoy representation of their own perspectives on aspects of schooling and to participate in decisions about their schooling, as well as participating in global social interaction more widely. MAPs was an appropriate site to explore representation, given the unwavering commitment of MAPs teachers to the children's wellbeing. A short film (UCL Institute of Education, 2021) was made about the workshops and research project, which is available online.

How we ascertained the thoughts and feelings of Syrian refugee children at MAPs

We explored in great depth how schooling was experienced subjectively by diverse individual children, interrogating their beliefs and perspectives and engaging with them through activities that allowed them to express even views that were hard to articulate. Our interpretivist stance meant that we did not look for an external truth in the children's narratives but accepted that each narrative was their version of the truth, believing that how schooling is perceived and represented varies from

Figure 4.7 'My family' by a Syrian refugee pupil at a MAPs education centre.
© The authors.

one person to the next and that each narrative sheds light on its truth. Overall, as a research team, we asked the question: *How do displaced Syrian children experience schooling and social justice at MAPs learning centres in Beqaa and Arsal, Lebanon?*

The children we worked with

There were 45 children in our sample, which was drawn from the nine MAPs schools. Each of the schools had previously been invited to approach four children who might wish to attend the three-day data-collection workshop we were offering. The children were given full details and allowed to ask any questions about the project in advance. We did not specify any particular age group but most of the children who attended were from the top class of the primary school, usually either Grade 5 or 6 (aged 9–13), depending on the centre. Some schools sent more than four children, leading to a total cohort of 45. Unfortunately, however, five boys did not attend on the final workshop day. Participation in any activity was completely optional and any participant could stop at any time.

It is important to note that our aim in this book is to relay first-hand the experiences of some Syrian refugee children with whom we had the opportunity to engage. Our sample is not representative in any sense because it does not reach the many children who did not attend school at all or those who had dropped out of the provision, or those who were considered by their schools to be inappropriate to participate. Nor does our sample include those in schools managed by other charitable organisations. However, we draw here on a series of activities that were specifically facilitated to paint a picture that demonstrates how approaches to parity-of-participation can become meaningful for Syrian refugee children under certain conditions.

The process

Day 1: The children talked about their life-histories

On Day 1 of the project, in the first week of May 2019, we visited three MAPs school locations. The visits were an opportunity to meet 30 children from five different schools from the settlements in Beqaa (some of the children came in specially for the sessions from neighbouring schools). As a team of four researchers (who are also authors), we endeavoured firstly to get to know each group of children at each of the three school-sites and put them at ease. With the help of a MAPs translator, we explained the project fully to them and obtained their verbal consent to participate. We then invited them to fill in nine sentence-completions, explaining each one as they wrote and answering any questions they had. They all managed to complete the sentences and agreed to return to MAPs' central training centre/administration site the following day for the data-collection workshop. Meanwhile, a MAPs staff member followed the same process on our behalf in the four Arsal schools. We then asked for the finished sentence-completions to be translated immediately and sent to us to help us plan the next day's activities. The sentence-starters included the following, presented in Arabic, which was the community's native language:

1. The story of my schooling so far is like this: *[Mention all schools or classes you have attended, starting with the first; how you felt about each one; how each one helped you or not]*
2. The best thing about my lessons at school has been …
3. The type of lesson that I find most useful is …

4. Personal relationships and friendships have been important during school because ...
5. The most difficult thing about my lessons at school has been ...
6. In my ideal lesson, the teachers would ... *[List at least three ideals]*
7. What I have learnt at school will prepare me best for ...
8. I wish that school lessons had been better at ...
9. When I am an adult, I'd like to ... *[Any future ambition?]*

Day 2: The children talked more about their learning

We used a room within the MAPs headquarters at Beqaa and set it out café-style so that the children could sit comfortably, although it was not spacious. We began by showing them the film made mainly by previous MAPs children called 'Children of Hope' (Multi-Aid Programs, 2019, available at: https://youtu.be/Z7ZUOw0O_wk). One of the children in the film was at our research workshop, so we asked him to explain why and how that film was made. He told us that its aim was to reach far and wide and let the world know what MAPs children thought and felt about their education. We explained that our research aimed to do something similar.

Next, we carried out a mingling activity, by the end of which the children were mainly smiling or laughing and had mixed with those from other schools. We then invited each child to draw a picture of themselves doing what they hoped to be doing in five years' time (or longer if they liked). We then interviewed each child briefly about their pictures and audio-recorded their responses. Other audio data were gathered as we researchers listened in to their conversations and invited them to speak into the microphone if they were saying something of interest to our study. Across three days, we used this strategy during all activities.

After a break, we split the group into two. Each group had two MAPs office staff who translated for us and who were familiar to the children but not professionally invested in their learning trajectories. We asked the children to think back to their favourite learning activities during classes at school and to write answers to the following questions about those activities:

a) Describe exactly what you were doing during your favourite activity.
b) Describe what the teacher was doing during your favourite activity.
c) Describe how you felt about each part of the activity.
d) Describe the learning you got out of it.

e) What made this successful for you?

f) For next time, what would you like to add or change?

Finally, we asked each child to evaluate their experience so far in the research workshop by writing one evaluative sentence each. We collected these for analysis.

After a further break, we invited the children to write a certificate to someone who had helped them learn. We had printed out some formal certificate templates (in Arabic) for them to complete and take away with them, to present to the person concerned. Within the template, they wrote the person's name and then completed the following prompts:

> You helped me to learn because you …
> This was helpful to me because …
> The best thing you did for me was …

Finally, we invited the children to think back and discuss 'My favourite activity in the classroom', indicating on a sheet of paper the essential aspects that made each 'favourite activity' so special for them. We took photos of these sheets and then invited three small groups from the two larger groups to present their reflections to the rest of the children. These presentations were filmed.

Day 3: Writing to teachers

To start the third morning, we addressed the issue of 'recognition' directly but did so by centring on a very personal and individual level of 'recognition'. After modelling a recognition activity, we broke into our two groups again and, working in pairs, each child wrote down what they desired more recognition for, shared this with their partner, and then attempted to recognise their partner in the ways requested. Next, working individually, children wrote a letter to future teachers, starting with 'Dear Teachers, for your future students, we would like you to …' (some of which appear in this book). Then they wrote letters to future children, starting with 'Dear future students, to have the best possible learning experiences with your friends and teacher, we really encourage you to …'

Before the midday break, we invited each child to write about 'The best thing about this research workshop was …' and 'The hardest thing about this research workshop was …', as a final evaluation.

There were 36 children who completed these and handed them in. Meanwhile, our camera team, led by Annelise Andersen from UCL, was conducting one-to-one video interviews with eight children and two teachers, equally split between males and females. These individuals were chosen on the basis of the particular enthusiasm they had displayed during activities.

In the afternoon, 25 of the children's teachers attended the final ceremony. The children sat facing the teachers, and those children who wanted to were encouraged to read out their 'letter to future teachers'. Each child then presented their letter, in an envelope, to a teacher of their choice. Those who did not want to read them out just presented their letters. The teachers seemed engaged and supportive throughout the children's presentations. After the workshop had ended, we stayed in touch with one child whom we have called Raghida. She showed particular interest in our work and later wrote a brief life-history (displayed at the start of the Introduction) which we translated and analysed along with the rest of the data.

Analysis

One of the researcher/author team, a native speaker from Syria, transcribed and translated all the written and audio data, including the

Figure 4.8 'My house on the Lebanese border' by a Syrian refugee pupil at a MAPs education centre. © The authors.

interview scripts. She then cross-checked her translations with another native speaker from Syria. We took this textual data and read it through, identifying and coding relevant themes or those that kept arising. We endeavoured to allow these to emerge organically, rather than deciding in advance what we might expect. We then re-read the documents, successively reapplying these codings and developing them further in a similar fashion. After refining the codings over several iterations, we identified nine emerging themes, which underpin and inform the sub-headings discussed next. Collaboratively, as a team of authors, we then made conceptual links between the final codings and the components of Fraser's and Kohli's theories, in order to position our research data within the framework of social justice and, specifically, the barriers to refugee education.

Throughout the process, in terms of ethical considerations, we were strongly guided by Lenette's (2019) conceptualisation of refugee participants as 'knowledge-holders' rather than passive suppliers of information. Ethical issues were particularly sensitive in this research, for two important reasons. First, we were engaging with young people who were vulnerable. We had to meet their needs and engage with them in ways that suited them, requiring us to emphasise that the process was entirely voluntary and that they could leave at any time. In gaining children's verbal and written consent, we explained in writing and verbally on several occasions what the project would entail before asking them to sign up for it. Second, we were investigating an emotive topic that needed to be handled with great care for both the children and their teachers. As we did not wish to cause harm by inviting the children to focus on their own suffering, we stressed that we were inviting them to share their perspectives because the wider world would like to hear them. We followed British Sociological Association guidance on ethical procedures and had clearance from the UCL Institute of Education Ethics Committee.

Turning to the nine themes we identified, in alphabetical order, these were: 1) Admiration and respect for teachers; 2) Becoming something great in the future; 3) Caring and collaboration; 4) Curriculum needs and provision; 5) Focus on grades and teacher explanation; 6) Justice and social awareness; 7) Pain, fear and suffering; 8) Preferences in learning; and 9) Syria. These informed the themes that are captured in the sub-headings that follow.

The children's sense of belonging to the global Syrian community

The children's sensibility toward people's suffering at a global level seemed more advanced than might otherwise have been expected if they had not been displaced by war. Despite their assumed low status in global policy discourses (Pinson & Arnot, 2007), their global awareness and sense of belonging to an afflicted Syrian community subjected to complex world events was worthy of note, albeit in rather a tragic sense (see Figure 4.8 for their awareness of the border between Syria and Lebanon). Their desire and will to act compassionately in response to these people's fate were also clear. For example, one child talked about the importance of helping those in the world who were drowning as they sought refuge. Another mentioned helping the wounded from the battlefield. Yet another's ambition was 'to start a garden with my friends for children to play in' while several others aspired to become doctors 'to help cure dying children ... who are bleeding', as one child phrased it (see Figures 4.9 and 4.10 regarding the dream of becoming doctors; and Figure 4.11 regarding the aspiration to attend university one day).

Another child recognised how important it was to have interactions with others in our community to 'improve society' because, she

Figure 4.9   'My goal in the future is to be a doctor' by a Syrian refugee pupil at a MAPs education centre. © The authors.

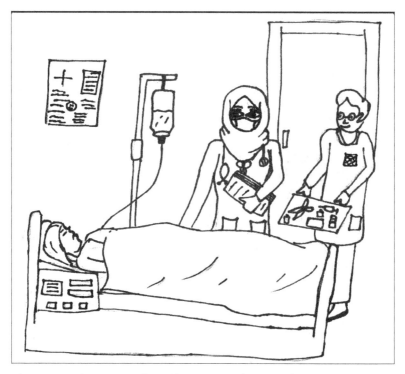

Figure 4.10 'Becoming a doctor' by a Syrian refugee pupil at a MAPs education centre. © The authors.

commented, 'as we grow up, the society around us evolves'. It appears that the children used their sense of belonging to the Syrian people everywhere to cultivate a strong will to contribute in the future to society, and to their Syrian society in particular.

These findings suggest that the sample children were already acquiring a sense of global responsibility toward other Syrians who were suffering, despite their own limited safety and sense of belonging in their immediate context of Lebanon. They seemed to see the global picture of the Syrian community and to want to contribute to improving life for other Syrians who were even more unfortunate than them. Not only did these children adhere to the Syrian community worldwide but it was striking also how much value they placed on their immediate friends (see Figure 4.12) and their collaborations with them within the safety of the MAPs community.

Their geographical exclusion from both the homeland and the host country seemed to strengthen the mutual bonds they

Figure 4.11 'In ten years, I'd like to be a university student. God will guide me' by a Syrian refugee pupil at a MAPs education centre. © The authors.

Figure 4.12 'Friends' by a Syrian refugee pupil at a MAPs education centre. © The authors.

felt with their peers. In addition, it is worth considering that their physical isolation in very confined spaces may have rendered those bonds even closer. Raghida wrote in her short life-history document:

> In my school, I had friends who weren't just friends but sisters … My friends and I were the best of friends because we spent [so much] time together, playing and studying together.

Then she went on to explain that she and some of her friends had been separated because the MAPs schools did not have sufficient funding to provide education beyond Grade 5 (age 9+). Separation seemed to be an especially pertinent issue among some of these children that perhaps threatened their sense of safety and belonging. Raghida told us that two of her best friends had moved away:

> We separated from our other friends, K and A, who went far away to other parts of the country. We all used to live in the same camp, but now we don't. K cannot come to visit us anymore, but A does come every now and then.

It makes intuitive sense that, when suffering from the unjust distribution of material wealth and from low status in national and global eyes, children would come to depend heavily on building relationships among themselves – and also their families – as a means to construct a sense of safety and belonging (see Figures 4.13 and 4.14, both entitled 'My family', by two Syrian refugee children attending the MAPs schools).

When we asked the children to evaluate the three-day research workshop, at least 16 out of the 36 told us that making friends with others like themselves (that is, other displaced Syrian children) was the best part of the experience:

> The best thing about this research was the sharing, the collaboration and the friendship; and [the fact] that I took part in [it].

Here, the child appreciated making friends and also the sense of being a valued part of a common venture. With no opportunity to collaborate as socially recognised members of society either in their home country or the host country, collaborating among fellow displaced children perhaps helped satisfy their human right to

Figure 4.13 'My family' by a Syrian refugee pupil at a MAPs education centre.
© The authors.

participation and enhanced their sense of belonging to this specific community. This may explain why so many children emphasised their delight at being allowed to collaborate and make more friends during the research workshop.

When asked to reflect on any learning activity they had engaged in during the research and tell us what their key learning or main success from it was, at least half the children's written comments described making new or extended friendships. This theme is illustrated in the following written examples:

> I learned love and friendship.
> I felt I was making my friends happy, and they helped me.
> What made it successful was me making new friends.

Several children accompanied thoughts about collaboration with concepts including love, honesty, loyalty and sincerity, qualities that were conducive to feeling safe and having a sense of belonging.

Figure 4.14 'My family' by a Syrian refugee pupil at a MAPs education centre. © The authors.

One child called this 'the spirit of good treatment between friends'. When asked what made their learning successful, another child wrote:

> Dedication, sincerity, appreciation for each other, collaboration and honesty between people.

At one stage in the research workshop, we asked the children to give advice to future MAPs pupils. Many advised them to treat each other well. For example:

> Treat each other with love and friendship.
> I hope you will cooperate and [show] each other the best treatment.
>   Be good and respect honesty.

This spirit of goodwill is in stark contrast with, for example, the nationalist discourse manifested in the Lebanese citizenship education curriculum that promotes social exclusion and limits critical and dialogic pedagogies (Akar & Albrecht, 2017; see also Chapter 2). Indeed, in their own way, the children in our study particularly emphasised dialogic pedagogy and how this could support their learning. One child, for instance, wrote: 'Collaboration guarantees success'. It seems that some children perceived collaboration with their peers during the workshop to assist their learning by inspiring new ideas (as well as by making the activity more sociable). When asked what made a learning task successful, one child wrote:

> Collaborating in friendship and love and exchanging opinions and ideas ... That made the whole thing successful for me.

Another wrote:

> I felt happy because we were collaborating and generating ideas.

Yet a third child recommended to teachers:

> Add some more fun and time and love to enhance the collaboration between us, so that our lesson becomes better and more special.

The children sometimes showed signs of self-direction in their approach to learning, which was perhaps a surprising finding given the authoritarian nature of schooling in their home country (see Chapter 6). For example, during our sessions, one child advised another how to learn to do division better:

> Try to learn it at home, and then come back to ask the teacher. Use YouTube! Search: 'How to divide'. Or just ask your sister or someone who knows how, and you will be able to divide.

There were other written examples of children emphasising their self-directed will to succeed in their learning:

> I learned that I should not depend on anyone else, and depend on myself.
> I learned how to think and to be quick and to be confident.
> I learned the ability to imagine and think about the future.

One child told us about the usefulness of the learner teaching the lesson to another learner, an additional feature of dialogic pedagogy that is likely to contribute further to feelings of safety and belonging within the community:

> The best thing that I liked about this lesson was that the teacher used to get the students to re-explain the lesson after he finished teaching us.

Another aspect of pedagogy focused on by the children was its inclusive nature, suggesting that they were aware of how to reinforce community. Several children asked teachers not to discriminate negatively against any MAPs children '[b]ecause all people are the same', as one child explained. Another child requested of her teacher: 'I hope you treat students fairly inside and outside the classroom'. Fairness seemed to imply, for them, not discriminating between children and taking care of 'all students equally'. This is another aspect of pedagogy that does not always receive sufficient attention in traditional classrooms, where those children who find schoolwork easier can be singled out for preferential treatment while those who struggle have a lower status and perhaps sit nearer the back. The children in our sample, however, specifically mentioned paying equal attention to those who struggled with their learning alongside those who were more successful. They also recognised the need to look after the smaller children at school. However, of course, this was only within the particular groups of children served by the MAPs schools, and the orientation might have been different if other groups had been included. We can only hypothesise that this sense of needing to make all feel belongingness derived from the children's own need to belong and the lurking fear of not belonging in the host country. Of course, this could also work in the opposite direction if different groups were added, whereby a sense of inequality could lead to conflict among the unequal groups (Novelli et al., 2019).

However, this latter scenario was not relevant among our partici-pants as they all seemed to consider themselves part of the MAPs community of nine camps, despite having originally lived in a range of different situations and villages in Syria.

One particularly relevant aspect of this emphasis on belonging was some children's explicit request to have their experiences represented, including to teachers. In their evaluations of the three-day research workshop, comments that illustrated their appreciation of having their views heard included the following:

> The best thing about being part of this research was sharing my perspectives with everyone, with the pupils and with the teachers.

One of the teachers, during the interview, captured the collabora-tive nature of this community that was less hierarchical than might be expected in other school contexts. She explained that she had decided to actually act on the children's requests, to show that they were, indeed, heard:

> The first thing we [teachers] will do is to consider the students' suggestions and integrate them into our teaching practice ... I will tell them that expressing their thoughts and opinions is their legitimate right and a right of every child. They can do that constantly.

Another teacher commented:

> We can design and conduct activities that allow them to express how they feel, so this becomes routine practice and the child becomes used to expressing their feelings towards anyone and anything, not just their teachers ... this is a positive thing, and we welcome such an approach.

These collaborative, dialogic, inclusive approaches would be surprising among children in other countries who followed traditional teaching methods – such as those previously employed in Syrian Government schools (see Chapter 7). Perhaps the urgent needs for safety and belonging, which were highlighted by the continuing temporariness of these children's lives, encouraged them to think more collaboratively.

The children admired and respected teachers who championed a sense of safety and belonging

Both in their recorded words and also when we observed them interacting in person with the teaching staff, the children's true affection and admiration for their teachers were striking (see Figures 4.15–4.17). These feelings seemed to be reciprocated. It may be that this closeness was another outcome of the children's and teachers' mutual awareness of the need to hold onto feelings of safety and belonging. Some children also told us that they wanted to become teachers when they grew up.

Here is a glowing testimony, contained in one child's letter to her teachers, which she read out to them on the last day of our research workshop:

Figure 4.15 'My teacher at school' by a Syrian refugee pupil at a MAPs education centre. © The authors.

Figure 4.16 'In my class' by a Syrian refugee pupil at a MAPs education centre. © The authors.

Figure 4.17 'The job I want to do when I grow up' by a Syrian refugee pupil at a MAPs education centre. © The authors.

I learned that the teacher is an essential pillar of our lives, and without teachers, life is incomplete.

Another described how her happiness was linked to her teacher's:

I felt really happy because the teachers were happy, and when I see my teachers happy, I feel so much happiness.

Another typical expression of appreciation was exemplified by a certificate of thanks that one of the children gave to their teacher, in which the child linked the teacher's commitment to her own enhanced will to succeed:

I want to give this certificate to my teacher Hanan. You helped me learn because you have faith in me and are devoted to helping me. That was useful for me because education helps in building one's future. The best thing you offered me was learning and education, which are very important in life!

There were many qualities in their teachers that the children admired. Smiling was important, as was being good-natured with the children as it helped them feel safe. One child requested of future teachers that 'you'd always smile so that you'd be an encouragement to us'.

Many children described and appreciated the gentle kindness and understanding that their teachers displayed, as witnessed when the children presented their letters to the teachers in our final session of the research workshop. Given the traumas they had experienced as displaced children, such gentle kindness and understanding were evidently helpful in providing the children with a sense of safety (see 'pedagogies of love' in Chapter 5). Raghida insightfully noticed how the best teachers were not only kind and compassionate but also helped children's learning by responding to how they were feeling in the moment:

Mr Mahmoud also became my favourite and best teacher because he was extremely considerate of our feelings. Thus, if he noticed that we were bored, he would teach the lesson through playing a game, so that we'd understand it and never feel bored during it … He is also a terrific teacher because he won't leave the class until he makes sure that all of us have understood the lesson well.

Pinson and Arnot (2007, p. 401) referred to the particular threats to safety these children had experienced and the 'complex needs of these [displaced] children in terms of personal, social health'. In their interviews, teachers mentioned the importance of being responsive to children's sensitivities during teaching because children were not only dealing with the subject matter but also emotional and social problems provoked by trauma:

> They all live in camps, so they lack many things. Hence, our methods in teaching them should differ from those followed in teaching other students. In order to compensate for the deprivation they are suffering, we should include activities in our practice that enhance their learning.

Teachers' encouragement was specified as particularly valuable, which was not surprising in an environment where fear and uncertainty were rife. Some children emphasised their sense of safety and belonging within MAPs schools by likening teachers to family, with one expressing: 'They are like fathers to us, and they are nice to us all.' Another said of her teacher: 'He treated us as if we were his little siblings.' This perhaps related to the fact that the teacher showed a genuine interest in the children and their aspirations in life or, as one child wrote, 'cared for me and for what's good for me' and was willing to work hard on the children's behalf. This suggests that the children especially value the encouragement given by teachers as a prop to their sense of safety; and this included taking the children's ambitions seriously.

A particularly unexpected characteristic of the teaching staff that was mentioned quite frequently by children was the gift some teachers had of bonding with their pupils in a mutually beneficial partnership. In an interview, one child told us:

> You see, if you as a student teach a teacher about a piece of information that is new to the teacher, this is a good thing, and the student will be delighted to do so ... They taught us so we should encourage them as well.

Another child admitted that this parity-of-participation in lessons was out of the ordinary:

> We [typically] feel afraid when we stand in front of them [teachers] and we tremble. They are older and we are younger,

but *we* are teaching *them*! Yet, they were our teachers and they were teaching us.

Such a partnership perhaps afforded the children a sense of participation in a safe environment in which their views were heard and acted on. One child spoke of his teacher as follows: 'He likes me, and I like him, and I constantly help him, and he helps me'. We can only speculate that experiencing this sense of being able to contribute to teaching, even teaching one's teachers, will be a crucially important skill for these children's futures, given the lack of social recognition they are currently being shown by the host-nation and the global community alike. A belief in their own worth as teachers and encouragers of others could boost their sense of social status as well as making it more likely that they will continue to seek to make their voices heard. If, as a start, these children were allowed to contribute to decisions that are being made about them as individual children – as Lundy (2007, p. 931) suggests – in time, this could facilitate their participation in school and classroom policies and, eventually, the formulation of government policy or UN statements.

The children expressed a need for a wider curriculum and more schooling

Some children, perhaps surprisingly in the circumstances, seemed to value criticality as a learning trait. Despite their admiration and respect toward teachers, the children in our study showed themselves to be quite capable of being critical of their teachers, for the benefit of future learners in their community. This perhaps illustrates the trust and sense of belonging they had acquired in the MAPs classrooms. Some children felt the need to apologise to their teachers for being critical but they couched their criticisms in such obviously loving terms that it would have been hard for any teacher to take offence. The children showed surprisingly deep insights into how they were taught and were able to make valid suggestions for improvements. For example, one child represented others when she proposed that people cannot learn if they do not feel looked after:

> We want teachers to treat students well and never be angry at them so that students can understand the lessons.

This willingness to critique perhaps also reflected their drive to succeed despite the unjust conditions. For example, they requested longer lessons and more time in school generally. This probably reflected the fact that MAPs as a charity did not have sufficient funding to provide a full curriculum or full days in school for all children, as noted earlier, and that the Lebanese Government was not willing to provide appropriate schooling for these Syrian refugee children (see Chapter 3). Their apparent will to succeed in the future drove them to anticipate possible negative consequences of their limited schooling. Within the wider society of Lebanon, they perceived their low status; but, within their own school community, they felt safe enough to express their desires. For example, one child told us:

> I would also like to have more lessons and extended sessions so that topics can be explained more thoroughly.

Another child wrote:

> The lesson would be better if it was longer and if there were more questions.

The children in our study described many areas of learning that they desired to tackle but were not part of the MAPs school curriculum and were not available to them through Lebanese schools' curricula. The following reflection from Pinson and Arnot's writing highlights this very point – that, although all children have the right to education, displaced children can be denied that right because they do not belong legally to the host nation-state. This was the case for the children in the MAPs settlements. To Lebanon's eyes, they had no 'right to have rights' (Arendt, cited in Fraser, 2008) within their refugee status. They had no right to be in Lebanon at all. They therefore forfeited their right to schooling unless benefactors such as MAPs stepped in to help them. Pinson and Arnot (2007, pp. 400, 405), referencing the work of Shaila Benhabib, capture this context thus:

> Modern states today … have to face the decision whether an individual's social rights should continue to be distributed according to *citizenship* or according to *personhood* … Globalisation, human mobility and forced migration have altered the traditional nation-state and disrupted modern regimes of rights.

However, for some subjects delivered by the MAPs education centres, the children lacked even core parts of school provision that are necessary to fulfil their rights to a quality education (SDG 4). They frequently mentioned their desire to have sports lessons, especially because of the link between sport and health, which was an important factor in their sense of safety. Geography, French, ethics, Qur'ān studies, story-telling and embroidery lessons were also requested. And several children asked for school trips that would take them out of the camp. This latter request was problematic to fulfil, however, as it was inadvisable for these children to travel in case they were arrested as illegal settlers.

Given their traumatic backgrounds and the tough conditions of their current existence, it does not surprise us that the children spoke of their need for fun, games and the use of humour in the learning of the curriculum. This, again, might contribute to their sense of safety and a welcome ordinariness in daily life. Giggling, one child told us:

> We had an English lesson and we learnt together and laughed; the most important thing is that we had fun!

A need for play was mentioned by several children, for example in requests for more break times and 'breaks filled with fun'. Such activities would surely contribute to their sense of returning to a safer, more 'ordinary' life where it was normal to play. One child drew a funfair when asked what she hoped to be doing in five years' time, implying that this was part of the 'ordinary' life she had left behind. She explained:

> I drew a funfair. In five years' time, my wish is to go to a nice funfair and play on the swings and slides.

At least a quarter of the children in the study requested that teachers inject more humour, fun and enjoyment into their lessons, perhaps as a recompense for other miseries suffered in their current situation or perhaps in the realisation that fun helped them learn better. Among their messages to teachers were the following requests:

> Dear teachers, I would like you to treat future students well and make the lessons more interesting … more fun and enjoyable.
> Dear teachers, please offer the students some fun in the classroom, so they don't get fed up during the lesson.

Others recommended using games to enhance learning and make the lesson more fun. A few children equated increased fun with 'new ways and methods in their teaching'. They wanted activity and novelty, perhaps illustrating their desire to progress and succeed like other people of their age group in the world. One child wrote: 'When we were done with one activity, I used to become very excited as we were starting a new activity'.

In an interview, one of the teachers recognised the children's need for fun, partly as an antidote to the suffering they had experienced:

> If teaching methods were developed to entail more play and other things, we would be tackling other issues that they [are having to deal with], like their psychological state or emotional state because they come from very difficult situations and they all live in camps, so they must have many needs.

The children asked for more supplies such as colouring pens and coloured paper but, again, the budget was limited and such items had become luxuries. In their evaluations of the three-day research workshop, therefore, the children expressed pleasure at the supplies we had brought with us and the fun, activity-based nature of our sessions. Our team's unthinking provision of 'ordinary' coloured paper and stickers contrasted with the children's delight and sense of luxury at using them.

The children in our study expressed a wide range of skills and interests including football, running, English, cooking, photography, drawing and painting, singing, computers and, strikingly, the act of learning itself (see Figure 4.18).

This challenges the 'stem the flow' rhetoric of national narratives of exclusion (Pinson & Arnot, 2007, p. 403). Kohli (2011) suggested that safety and a sense of belonging usually precede success, including in school subjects. The following comments from the children in relation to the love of learning itself illustrate a capacity for deep engagement in learning, possibly indicating the 'will' Kohli referred to. Two children had high praise for the act of learning maths:

> I love decimal numbers. They are excellent!
> I learned that decimal numbers are wonderful because I like multiplication and division.

One child felt excited about Arabic grammar:

> When my teacher used to enter the classroom, my friends and I used to feel excited, especially when we had a grammar lesson.

Figure 4.18 'My hobby' by a Syrian refugee pupil at a MAPs education centre. © The authors.

The teachers were aware of the children's thirst for learning. Teachers remarked in interview:

> The students have the will and desire to learn.
> The students have … asked for a summer school. I concluded that [they] do not want to stay at home, that they want to learn more and that they like their teachers.

Given that home was a structure made of plastic sheets, cardboard or pieces of wood, in which the whole family lived (see Figure 4.19),

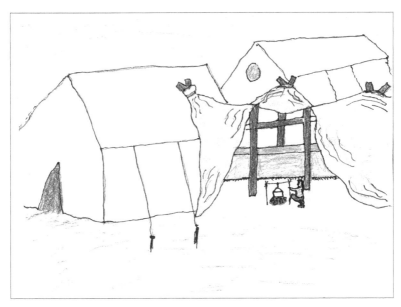

Figure 4.19 'Living in Lebanon' by a Syrian refugee pupil at a MAPs education centre. © The authors.

this preference for studying elsewhere was understandable but did, presumably, also benefit the children's learning.

However, in a situation where children live in such conditions but are *not* met by caring, valuing teachers in school, these conditions might have driven the children to engage in less productive ways to fill their time.

It is intriguing that the culture of examination preparation penetrated the MAPs schools, even though ultimately the children could not qualify within the Lebanese system or even be entered for the country's public examinations as they were denied this right, regardless of their assessment scores or academic progress (see Part 1 of this chapter). Despite the informal nature of the MAPs schools, the examination of curriculum material was still something to be feared, as one child explained:

> When they hand us exam papers and we have to start doing the exam, we become terrified.

The teachers emphasised the goal of children achieving high grades in examinations. However, the expressed emphasis in the MAPs schools on preparing children for a fulfilling future, rather than just good grades in examinations, seems contrary to the chosen focus on narrowly defined curricula and assessments. Until such time as refugees are in a position 'to take part in the consumerist game' (Pinson & Arnot, 2007, p. 404) typical of European countries, including the examination game, end-of-year examinations could be seen as wasting the precious learning time that children wanted to increase. Meanwhile, just as in meritocratic situations the globe over, those MAPs children who did well in examinations were very pleased with their achievements. One possible explanation for the children's and teachers' persistence with the examination culture could perhaps have been their desire to cling to those structures that were familiar from Syria and therefore reinforced a sense of still belonging there.

Longing to return to ordinary life in Syria – a home

Underpinning all the data lies an attachment to Syria, the home country of all the participating children and their teachers, even though some of the children were too young to remember it directly. They did not speak a lot about the war in Syria from which they and their families had fled; and one teacher commented in interview that they perhaps tried to protect themselves by avoiding thinking about it. He said: 'They never speak of [their pain] in the classroom, they never tell us how they feel'. However, the attachment to Syria – and the safety and sense of belonging it used to offer – was sustained and expressed in their writing. Raghida's narrative also illustrated the link between her hard work in the present and her ambition to return to Syria in the future. She wrote:

> I have never [forgotten] and will never forget my beloved country, Syria, and I will say it out loud so that everyone can hear it: my gratitude goes to my country, to the holy land that I was born in, my homeland, where I felt safe and secure. I am very proud of my country, which I cherish. Many thanks to my country, the land of goodness and generosity. I know that my words can never express what I feel for you and can never describe what you are really like. It is true that me and my friends have become separated from you now, but we promised ourselves, and hereby we promise you, that we will study, work hard and graduate to become worthy and important in the future, and that we will go back and build Syria together, as one hand.

Reference to returning to Syria was a common theme among the children; it seemed to be a general assumption that they would return one day.

In some senses, they were already preparing for that day; and, indeed, in collaborating with each other in anticipation of that day, they were reinforcing the sense of belonging that the idea of Syria gave them:

> The importance of helping each other, collaboration: we must help each other so all of us can [re-]build our destroyed country – and in order to help others as well.

The hostility these children were experiencing in their current environment and the distance (in time and kilometres) from the homeland seemed to drive their determination forward to prove their Syrian allegiance (see Figure 4.20, which illustrates their sense of the distance between Syria and Lebanon).

Given the injustices they were experiencing in terms of all three aspects of social justice – redistribution, recognition and representation – they would likely form a tight-knit community who opposed enemies on two sides (the Lebanese Government and the warring Syrian factions, respectively), rather than thinking about networks or contributions they themselves could make in Lebanon or other countries. Instead, the children talked about building a new Syria one day, in an imaginary future in which Assad would be vanquished and no longer control Syria.

Figure 4.20 'From Syria to Lebanon' by a Syrian refugee pupil at a MAPs education centre. © The authors.

However, Sidhu and Taylor (2007), among others, have warned that the abandonment of local communities such as these refugees in Beqaa and Arsal can lead to an increase in separatism and group enclaving rather than trans-group interaction. It was therefore not surprising that the children we spoke to felt entirely Syrian, with no sign of ambitions to make any links to Lebanese people or society. Since they could not travel, the children's own particular camp as part of MAPs seemed to have become their community, ostensibly keeping them safe against those who sought to harm them until such a time as they could return home. One child, describing the hope encapsulated by another child's drawing in Figure 4.21, wrote:

> In five years' time, we will go back to Syria and build our houses, and the seeds we planted before going to Lebanon will have grown up.

The following quote is beautifully representative of many children's aspirations. Some hoped to become engineers or architects to help rebuild Syria after the war. This particular child expressed how careers in construction were therefore the most important (see Figure 4.22):

Figure 4.21 'My home in Syria in ten years' by a Syrian refugee pupil at a MAPs education centre. © The authors.

Figure 4.22 'We are going back to Syria, with God's help' by a Syrian refugee pupil at a MAPs education centre. © The authors.

An artist is making a lot of money now, for sure; but tomorrow, when we get back to our homeland, I am sure the artist won't be that important. However, tomorrow [the near future], an engineer, for example, will construct many buildings and build the homeland and become proud that he built the country and became an architect.

Another child could envisage the power of becoming a writer to describe and represent their situation and disseminate this description:

> A human being wishes for many things, and dreams of becoming a doctor, an engineer or a teacher in the future; and they will do whatever God intends for them. [As for me], I dream of and wish to become a famous writer who writes stories for young and old people. I want to write about how we used to live in our safe and sound and beautiful country. Suddenly, I do not know what happened. We lost everything, we lost our country, our dreams – and we became [stranded] in the country of refuge. I will write to explain how much we suffered and how much we miss our country and our neighbours. I will write about all of that! I will also tell them how we studied and learnt, because when we return to our country, with God's will, we will hold its head high [we will make our country proud] and we will grant our country prosperity and wealth. I wish to become a writer and return to my beautiful country!

In the meantime, despite attempts by teachers to counter such views, the children believed that some Lebanese people did not welcome Syrian refugees – a belief that threatened their sense of safety and belonging in Lebanon. They referred occasionally to their own fate as stateless and status-less people (Pinson & Arnot, 2007), denied the right to fair status-recognition or representation. They recognised how current Lebanese policy was, indeed, 'systematically depreciating some categories of people and the qualities associated with them' (Fraser, 2008, p. 26). One child told us:

> I am proud of being Syrian but no one appreciates that. Because the Lebanese do not appreciate the Syrians, I end up feeling that Syrians are worthless.

In interview, one child referred to the injustice of Syrian children not being able to belong to Lebanese schools:

> Those who are not going to school should be able to go to school. There are many schools that do not accept Syrians. We should be allowed to fulfil our dreams! Specifically, we should be allowed to go to school in order to fulfil our dreams.

The children's awareness, in these statements, of some aspects of national and global politics, and their stated aims to improve these, would also render them well-placed to contribute to international decision-making in the future.

A strong will to succeed, despite significant setbacks

The children's marked will to succeed was possibly boosted by the setbacks they had had to overcome. For example, while some international policies recognise that refugees have high levels of resourcefulness and resilience due to their arduous experiences, others are prone to depicting them as weak victims who are dependent on others' help (Keddie, 2012). However, the children's own testimony contradicts this 'weak victim' image, and their powerful words could enlighten any policymakers who had access to them and an interest in them.

One child, for instance, noted how it was especially important that he and his peers learned well at school, given the high number of Syrian children who could not attend school at all, which would negatively affect Syria's future more generally. Other children made links between what they were learning at school and the individual success they hoped to achieve, illustrated by Figure 4.23:

> We are learning something now and we are happy that, when we grow up, in the future, we will be something big.

Many children had defined specific careers they were aiming toward, through studying in school now:

> In Maths, during the 'circle circumference' lesson, [a teacher] was teaching me how to measure any circle I find; and he helped me with my future and my life so that I can become an architect [one day], which will help me.

When the children wrote letters to their teachers, one of them conveyed the following message:

> You helped me to learn because you wanted me to become a doctor to help people … The best thing you gave me was your encouragement and [the fact that you made it clear] that you loved me.

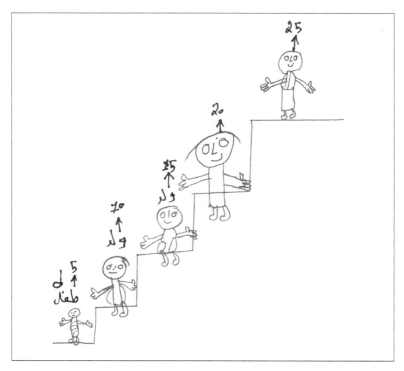

Figure 4.23 'Growing older' by a Syrian refugee pupil at a MAPs education centre. © The authors.

According to another child, teachers 'kept encouraging us to become what we want in the future', which perhaps gave the children the impetus to persevere in their studies as well as their ambitions. Another cited the Syrian proverb 'a day *for* you and a day *against* you', referring to life's vicissitudes. This proverb is used to urge people to save for an uncertain future or, equally, to be optimistic in bad times. The children were aware that they needed to acquire an education to secure a job in the unknown future. As one child exclaimed, 'If the person lives without having a job, what was he created for in this life?!' Given their circumstances, they may well have witnessed first-hand how hard it was for people to find employment. The lack of safety in this current national setting seemed to drive the children forward rather than depress them, perhaps *because* they enjoyed the safety of their MAPs schools. And, yet, the parents of the children we were working with did not enjoy equal opportunities to find the esteem conferred by employment as they were banned from all jobs in Lebanon except farming and construction. The children were likely to have been painfully aware of these limited

Figure 4.24 'Education is life' by a Syrian refugee pupil at a MAPs education centre. © The authors.

Figure 4.25 'Education is light' by a Syrian refugee pupil at a MAPs education centre. © The authors.

opportunities; indeed, one child wrote directly to the authors, asking for money in light of her father having no work. Education, for them, was a basic human right and the most important route to a successful future (see Figures 4.24 and 4.25).

Fortunately for these children, their will to succeed was coupled with their access to a safe, inclusive education provided by charitable donors, which afforded them at least a minimum of safety and belonging.

Reflecting on displaced children's experiences of social justice and learning

Our study set out with the aim of exploring the very broad research question: *How do displaced Syrian children experience schooling and social justice at MAPs learning centres in Beqaa and Arsal?* Our purpose was to provide an opportunity for these displaced children to reflect on and express their perspectives, and thus have their realities represented. Our purpose was also to convey these perspectives to their own teachers, to their future educators, and to a wider, global audience, sharing their ideas for improvement. Through this, we aimed to enhance this audience's knowledge and potential for activism. These purposes accorded with our focus on social justice as parity-of-participation including redistribution of wealth, recognition of status and – most importantly here – representation of perspectives (Fraser, 2008).

As outlined in Chapter 2, Ravi Kohli (2011) suggested that displaced children were likely to experience three primary (interrelated) needs: 1) safety, 2) a sense of belonging and 3) success. However, it is only when Fraser's three dimensions of social justice are enacted that we can fully meet these needs. A sense of safety will facilitate a sense of belonging, which, in turn, will support success. If, and only if, these needs are met, children are more likely to feel comfortable enough to represent their needs and views unprompted. Until that time, exceptional efforts will need to be made to elicit their reactions, such as those presented in this chapter.

Usually, the pursuit of safety starts with seeking the legal right to settle in the 'host' country. In the case of the Syrian children attending MAPs schools, however, despite not having any legal right to remain in their temporary settlements, some sense of safety appeared to be achieved in the schools through personal and social means alone. The children were not safe in physical terms: their shelters were temporary and could be destroyed at any time; their parents' livelihoods were volatile; and their futures were uncertain. And, yet, as we have seen in this chapter, their comments suggest they felt a level of safety and belonging due to the care and community they described experiencing among teachers and peers alike. Their peers' and teachers' shared life-histories of migration and oppression, their shared perception of not belonging in Lebanon, and their common love of their Syrian homeland appeared to create a bond between them in a mutually respectful MAPs community. Expressions of love between and among them and their teachers were striking to us as researchers; their thirst for learning and capacity for hard work were also quite extraordinary; and their social spirit of loyalty and honesty toward each other in achieving their ambitions was outstanding.

This safety and sense of belonging among people who actually lacked physical safety and did not belong in the host country seemed to drive their powerful will to succeed at school in order to be adequately equipped to return to the homeland and start to reconstruct it. In addition, the children had acquired many and varied talents despite their tough conditions, including a very high standard of writing in Arabic, mathematical competence, artistic and physical skills and many others. These were not the weak victims portrayed in some depictions of refugee children. Indeed, achieving this positive, community outlook was among the aims of the MAPs schools, and the children's representations suggested that this aim was being achieved, at least at the time of the research. As the situation in Lebanon has deteriorated since then, however, it is possible that their hopes and fears have shifted.

There is a challenge here as to whether this community spirit will thrive in a wider society which may be composed of people from other communities who have not experienced the same hardships and sense of togetherness as these children. Given their observation that the Lebanese Government did not value them and that the Assad regime in Syria wanted to destroy them, there could be a danger that these children become insular in the global context, seeking to cling to the community that offered them safety and participation and fearful of social interaction across other communities. This is a particular concern that necessitates urgent global action to link these communities in social interaction with other global communities. Their lack of realistic opportunities to continue in education only adds to this isolation, of course, and risks further separatist enclaving.

Final thoughts on representation

In terms of our key focus, representation as a mechanism of political justice, we acknowledge that, in the global policy discourses of many countries (including Lebanon), refugee children tend to be unseen.

According to Keddie (2012), policies place them at a significant disadvantage, illustrating social injustice. Our concern for promoting the representation of their lived experiences stemmed from the fact that, in Article 2 of the UNCRC, representation is listed as the right of every child 'without discrimination of any kind, irrespective of the child's or his or her parent's … national, ethnic or social origin'. Our findings illustrate that, because of the safety and belonging they found at the MAPs schools, the children in our sample were, to some extent, learning how to articulate their own perspectives at school, how to engage in critical dialogue and how to present themselves in a confident and self-determined way. These attributes are likely to support their future struggles to be heard and have their perspectives acted on. We have shown that their teachers were supportive of this right and that, following the research carried out in this project, some actually built it into their pedagogies more systematically (see Chapter 7).

However, our findings also made it very clear that the refugee children's right to a quality education in Lebanon, which should be 'available, accessible, acceptable and adaptable to all' (Tomasevski, 2001), was not being respected. The children's pleas for more school, longer lessons, more subjects, summer courses and more homework were clear evidence of the poor distribution of resources and poor recognition of status among these motivated young people. They themselves recognised that these injustices would not only disadvantage them as individuals but would also disadvantage the future of Syria and thereby international relations. SDG 4 – inclusive and equitable education and lifelong learning opportunities for all – was clearly far from being fulfilled in this situation.

APPENDIX C

C.1 The Sentence Completion activity

The best thing about school is: Nothing

The worst thing about school is: School

I learn best when: I am alone

I cannot learn when: I am tired الحالة النفسية → (psychological state)

In class, I sometimes think of: المستقبل → (Future)

My best memory is: my childhood in my grandfather's house.

My worst memory is: leaving my country

For me, the best subject is: 3D because: It's fun.

and the worst subject is: Maths because: the teacher.

The best teacher is one who: respects me.

The worst teacher is one who: disrespects me.

For better learning, I suggest: good relationships with teachers

If I were a teacher, I will: I will understand everyone's sutuation

Figure 5.1 Questionnaire response from a Syrian refugee pupil in London.
© The authors.

15-year-old Sultan: 'I just know I don't belong here …'

5
Representations of Syrian refugee children in an Inner London school: Case study 2

Introduction

Through this second case study, we narrate the educational experiences of Syrian refugee children in an Inner London school. Albeit in an entirely different context from Lebanon, this chapter aims to broaden our understanding of what social justice as parity-of-participation might represent to another group of Syrian refugees in another displacement setting. Here, Syrian refugee children have begun to resettle in a very different cultural milieu. Although they appear to benefit from settling into what is perceived as a new and stable (permanent) home, we draw attention to and reflect on the points of alignment between their experiences and those of refugees in fragile settlements (exemplified by Lebanon).

In Part 1 of this chapter, we describe the situation of Syrian refugee children in English schools in relation to access and policies. We offer a glance at the hardships and obstacles they can face while attempting to access education in the UK. We also present a more in-depth review of Fraser and Kohli's concepts, previously outlined in Chapter 2, and describe the participants and research processes in the London study. In Part 2, we narrate the Syrian children's representations of their understanding of social justice in their particular schooling context and their experiences of learning and adapting to their school as well as their requests to their teachers.

Syrian refugee children's schooling in England

After more than 12 years of conflict in Syria, the Syrian refugees' exodus is perceived to be the world's largest. Of more than 14 million displaced Syrians, half are children: 6.8 million were displaced internally and 5.5 million fled to the five neighbouring countries (UNHCR, 2023). In the UK, 20,300 Syrian refugees were resettled under the Vulnerable Persons Resettlement Scheme (VPRS) between 2014 and 2020, and a further 3,700 applied for asylum in 2022 (Loft et al., 2023). Compared to the situation of Syrian refugees in Lebanon, Syrian refugees who resettled in the UK are perceived to be in a more favourable situation, with social support arrangements offered specifically to those who came under the VPRS and all Syrian children entitled to schooling. Nevertheless, Syrian refugee and asylum-seeking children and their families face different levels of difficulty and delays when trying to access education.

To begin with, the reported number of Syrian (among other) refugee and asylum-seeking (RAS) children enrolled in schools in England is neither reliable nor accurate. This is largely attributed to the lack of government documentation or an assigned department to collate data on RAS children (McIntyre et al., 2020). Moreover, children's immigration status is not required to be collected by schools for the national Pupil Level Annual School Census (PLASC) (Pinson et al., 2010, p. 253). This lacuna is also associated with the lack of a specific education policy to address matters of access, inclusion and education delivery for RAS children. Rather, their access and entitlement to education are seen as the responsibility of local education authorities and covered under Every Child Matters and other general educational policies that are not specific to the education of new arrivals (McIntyre et al., 2020; Pinson et al., 2010).

Although some argue that the absence of RAS children from UK education policy can assist integration (see Pinson et al., 2010), it has contributed to a lack of clarity on the processes and steps that schools ought to take when educating RAS children. This absence also encourages blanket responses that schools attempt to implement individually, rather than carefully designed procedures coordinated between schools that can address the needs of different groups of RAS children. Untailored responses have also been exacerbated by trends toward 'academising' schools (McIntyre et al., 2020). The fact that RAS children are not specifically reflected in educational policy may also explain the lack of dedicated funding and resources to help schools accommodate such children and 'support [their] cluster of economic, health, emotional and social as well as educational needs' (Pinson et al., 2010, p. 253). Schools and local educational authorities are mostly left to seek resources from general government funding including free school meals (FSM) and Pupil Premium (PP) grants. Asylum-seeking children are eligible for FSM and the PP under the Immigration and Asylum Act 1999. However, refugee children only receive the PP when facing specific circumstances or certain criteria are met, including if their families have been in receipt of benefits or if they are being looked after by their Local Authority (DfE, 2023). According to the UK Department for Education guidance on the PP (EEF, 2023, p. 3), this funding is allocated to schools for use in: a) providing the means necessary, including professional development, to achieve high-quality teaching, b) providing means of 'targeted academic support', such as tutoring, and c) deploying wider plans and strategies to tackle 'non-academic barriers to success in schools, such as attendance, behaviour and social and emotional support'. Schools can decide which children these regulations apply to.

Undoubtedly, equitable, inclusive and quality education is a human right to which all RAS children are entitled in their resettlement contexts (United Nations, 2015). In England, the law states that RAS children aged 5–18 have exactly the same entitlement to full-time, compulsory education as their English peers across Local Authority schools, academies and free schools. However, the reality is that these 'rights are experienced differently' (McIntyre et al., 2020, p. 392) because children who have been granted refugee status are more likely to be in full-time schooling than asylum-seeking children (Pinson et al., 2010; Anderson et al., 2004). Additionally, admission criteria can sometimes be specific to schools and local councils, although they should apply to all children including RAS pupils. The general premise is that local councils offer advice on the schools in the area where children can attend. Nevertheless, for many reasons, not all schools accept RAS learners. Among other issues, this could be to do with the availability of English as an Additional Language (EAL) provision, the availability of trained teachers, and the fear that refugee children will lower national and international exam results. For RAS children, this situation can mean long delays in accessing education after arriving in the UK. In that sense, these children are being perceived as a problematic burden and therefore must navigate extra layers of bureaucracy and administration to gain what should be equitable access to education (Pinson et al., 2010).

Once the child has secured access to a school place, the school proceeds to accommodate them in the mainstream system based on their English language proficiency. However, some of the Syrian RAS children have had their education either disrupted or discontinued due to the war and displacement. Furthermore, because some of these children do not have the necessary documentation that could help in assessing their prior education, capital and capabilities, they are often automatically designated to focus mainly on learning English and spending substantial time in EAL support units, hindering their potential access to the full curriculum. Additionally, once they are allocated to mainstream classes, they are often treated as one homogeneous group and placed in lower-attaining sets, which they might not leave until their school education ends. This being the case, the needs and capabilities of RAS children are mostly overlooked or go unrecognised, which can have long-lasting implications for their welfare, attitudes to learning, and overall progress (McIntyre et al., 2020).

The research with Syrian children in a London school

Like our research in the MAPs schools, this London-based study aimed to address the following question: *How do Syrian refugee children in England represent their understandings of social justice as parity-of-participation in relation to, and through, their schooling experiences?*

The research activities in this case study offer a platform to a group of six young Syrian learners in London to share their experiences of resettling in a new, different and more stable host-country and becoming students in an English school. Through these activities, they also reflect on their journeys toward home-making and how these are shaped by the presence or absence of conditions for social justice as they conceptualise and perceive them. Mirroring other chapters in this book, this chapter is concerned with the children's own repre-sentations of their life-histories and accounts of their daily social and educational lives and encounters. Unlike their counterparts in Lebanon, the Syrian children in this study had been granted the legal right, along with their families, to remain in the host-country. Only one of the six participants had come to the UK through the VPRS scheme, and the rest through a family reunification process whereby one of their parents had previously claimed asylum and become a refugee in the country. This meant that most of them had had to endure a long waiting time in mediating displacement countries as they all confirmed leaving Syria during the very first years of the conflict. Moreover, those who had come via the reunification route experienced a longer waiting time to access education in the UK: six months to one year, compared to a three-month wait for the only participant who had come through the VPRS. The secondary academy school in which the study took place was predominantly devoted to serving a multicultural area of Inner London, where most families were from Black British, migrant, or refugee backgrounds. The area was also described by the children as having high levels of gang activity. According to the school, most pupils, including the Syrian refugees, were entitled to FSM and PP.

The young Syrian refugees involved in this research were aged 13–16 at the time of the study and had been at that academy school for more than two years before the research was conducted. Additionally, they had each established some sense of stability, having lived in England for up to five years. Only one of the participants had had continuous formal learning before coming to the UK, while others in the group described having either an interrupted education or little-to-no formal schooling in Syria and mediating countries. This was attributed to the conflict in their hometowns in Syria, where their schools either became damaged during battle or were completely destroyed. While the children were in the mediating countries, the limited and/or unstable learning was due to several factors, including not being able to afford to join the local schools or not being allowed to do so; having to work to support the family; or the poor standard of schools, where overcrowding and corporal punishment prevailed.

Our study followed the young Syrians' day-to-day lives in London, collecting and co-constructing their life-histories based on their testimonies and perceptions around their social life and learning in their academy school. The collected narratives stretched back to the start of the conflict in Syria and included their stories of displacement, their respective journeys, and their post-settlement lives in London, of which school and its accompanying social life occupied a huge part. For nine months (from November 2019 to March 2020, and from October 2020 to January 2021), on a bi-weekly and group/individual basis, Jumana met with four female and two male Syrian pupils to hear their respective stories. During the times when they all met together as a group, the children made reference to different past events encompassing their experiences of war, repeated displacement, and the several journeys they had had to make to find a safe final resettlement destination. They also defined their lives in light of their future dreams, aims and plans. Jumana also met the children individually for multiple, lengthy, one-to-one conversations about how school life shaped their everyday existence, relationships with their social circles and adaptation to the resettlement country.

Safety in schools and its link to a sense of belonging: The need for parity-of-recognition

Like the MAPs study, this study largely drew on Kohli's (2011) framework addressing the need for young refugees to regain a sense of home in their new countries of resettlement. Regarding the resumption of a sense of ordinariness, Kohli contends that the young refugees' journeys do not end at the borders of their host-countries but continue through three main trajectories: the search for safety, the growth of belonging, and the development of a will to succeed within their new environments (Kohli, 2011). The study mainly follows the lead of McIntyre and Abrams (2021) in understanding the interplay between Kohli's three trajectories within a moral framework of social justice as parity-of-participation (Fraser, 2008), stipulating that, for a sense of home to be regained, conditions of social justice as parity-of-participation need to be in place to facilitate feelings of safety and belonging and encourage a will to learn and progress.

The need to use Kohli's framework emerged in response to the children's testimonies, allowing us to explore how differently each child's needs for safety, belonging and success might be represented. The differences depended on the child's life-history and how these trajectories could shape and be shaped by the young Syrians' perceptions of the presence or absence of social justice – or participatory parity – in their socio-educational context. In that sense, the study offered a deeper examination of the notion of safety within the Syrian children's contexts. Alongside feelings of belonging and developing a will to succeed, the data from this study suggested that Kohli's term 'safety' not only applied in the sense of living in a physically safe host-country; and nor did the sense of safety necessarily lead to a sense of belonging; rather, other surrounding relationships and the perceived absence of elements of social justice played important and unpredictable roles in the equation.

Regaining a sense of ordinariness cannot solely be confined to finding a safe country of settlement. We observe this through the young Syrians' arguments that home-making is closely related to their being able to participate in their new host-environments on terms of parity, and that this entails a prolonged and complicated process. We can also observe that it requires socially-just conditions that allow these children to feel safe, included and appreciated. Therefore, the requirement for environments to be inclusive must be understood beyond mere spatial and legal safety, and considered through a lens of social justice that examines the relationships and opportunities of equal participation that refugee children experience within their everyday settings. Thus, relations of love and genuine concern for the wellbeing of equal fellow humans seem important accompaniments to legal safety requirements.

The Syrian children's testimonies in this study raised the following questions: Which types of safety might be sufficient to promote feelings of belonging? And what kind of safety is required for refugee children to grow back some much-needed 'webs of belonging', to use Kohli's (2011) term?

Kohli associated feeling safe with some forms of stable, just and inclusive relationships. In other words, seeking to restore a sense of home (or belonging) necessitates more than just the search for physical and 'official' safety in terms of everyday resources. These questions become more prominent in relation to the context of school. One can argue that safety is both a legal *and a moral* perquisite that all schools should endeavour to fulfil and provide to all students. Safe spaces in which to learn are perceived as vital for promoting all pupils' wellbeing and learning (Kutsyuruba et al., 2015) and supporting refugee children's sense of belonging and will to succeed – given that schools are meant to 'prepare young people precisely for membership of a society, for citizenship' (Pinson et al., 2010, p. 248). Hence, feeling safe can be understood as an outcome of enjoying free and equal relationships with significant adults and peers, where the refugee child experiences a healthy social status (Sidhu & Taylor, 2007). Baumeister and Leary (1995, p. 497) suggested that:

> [T]he belongingness hypothesis is that human beings have a pervasive drive to form and maintain at least a minimum quantity of lasting, positive, and significant interpersonal relationships. Satisfying this drive involves two criteria: First, there is a need for frequent, affectively pleasant interactions with a few other people; and, second, these interactions must take place in the context of a temporally stable and enduring framework of affective concern for each other's welfare. Interactions with a constantly changing sequence of partners will be less satisfactory than repeated interactions with the same person(s) …

The need for positive relationships in schools and other educational institutions has long been argued for in response to the criticism that education is increasingly perceived to focus on 'the technical aspects of teaching with less [emphasis] on its "human" aspects' (Velasquez et al., 2013, p. 162). Positive caring and affective relationships in educational settings, demonstrated by safe, loving, responsive and participatory environments (Cohen, 2001), have been seen as fundamental in predicting and influencing children's engagement and achievement, child and youth development, and social adjustment (Roorda et al., 2011; Thapa et al., 2013). The need for such relationships is even greater among children from disadvantaged backgrounds and those at risk academically, particularly asylum-seeker and refugee children (Arnot & Pinson 2005; Sidhu & Taylor, 2007; Due et al., 2016; Wilkinson & Kaukko, 2020), as illustrated by the MAPs schoolchildren represented in Chapter 4. Moreover, the significance of nurturing positive and caring relationships in schools that host refugee children stems from the assumption that schools play a major role in the refugee settlement process (Sidhu & Taylor, 2007) and are 'places where healing can happen' (McIntyre & Abrams, 2021, p. 20). As such, school is the very first environment in which refugee children start to build social relations and establish contact with peers and other adults on a daily basis when they attempt to resettle in another country.

As suggested in Chapter 2, parity-of-participation is facilitated when adults – including staff and teachers – adopt practices and provide spaces that recognise children's identities, experiences and individual strengths and allow them to represent their needs and share their knowledge in the school environment (Due et al., 2016; Velasquez et al., 2013). This was also vividly illustrated by the MAPs schoolchildren featured in Chapter 4. Numerous other studies have emphasised refugee children's own perceptions of the link between safety and positive relationships with teachers. Due et al. (2016) highlighted how students felt safe as a result of having caring relationships with their classroom teachers and other staff. Virtanen et al. (2009) referred to students whose teachers offered them opportunities for participation in the classroom as expressing improved wellbeing and school attendance. Moreover, compassionate teachers played a major role in fostering students' sense of belonging and community at school (Velasquez et al., 2013).

These findings can be connected back to Kohli's framework, in which safety paves the way for refugee children to grow back webs of belonging 'as a mark of the progress of resettlement' (2006, p. xii). Kohli argued, based on several previous studies, that children could effectively use their agency and benefit from their past experiences to recreate their social and cultural webs and build back belonging, but that this process was predicated upon having access to supportive others who might offer safe and welcoming spaces for interaction as well as showing care. This notion resonates with arguments that a sense of mutual social recognition is essential in achieving belonging (May, 2015) and attaining social justice more broadly (Fraser, 2008; 2019). If every person were recognised as an equally valuable human being because of the cultural, social and personal strengths that they bring, this would contribute positively to fostering a sense of belonging.

Refugee children joining schools in their resettlement context – be it in England or any other resettlement country – need an inclusive, compassionate environment that values the cultural and social capital and experiences that they bring into their schooling (Pinson et al., 2010; McIntyre & Abrams, 2021). Indeed, Kaukko, Wilkinson and Kohli (2021, pp. 7–8) highlighted that the various stages of refugee children's settlement need to be accompanied by a 'range of pedagogical practices that can be attached to the notion of love' to assist children in 'developing feelings of safety and belonging, after which other types of success can follow'. The need to succeed is the third aspect of Kohli's framework of refugees' search for ordinariness. Upon establishing some sense of belonging, refugee children have been shown extensively to seek to succeed both educationally and materially. It is their way of proving that war can destroy anything *except* their will to live and prosper (Kellaway, cited in Kohli, 2011).

Importantly, McIntyre and Abrams (2021) point out that the resumption of ordinariness, according to Kohli's conceptualisation, does not occur in a vacuum. Instead, the paths that refugee children pursue to attain a sense of home are controlled and constrained by the acceptance or refusal of the prevalent social and political attitudes and policies. This means that achieving longer-term participation and success is influenced by the extent to which these young people are allowed to develop and participate in fruitful relationships within their everyday environments. Such an argument substantiates the need for a moral and normative conceptual framework of social justice within which the necessary material *and social conditions* can be investigated (see McIntyre & Neuhaus, 2021; McIntyre & Abrams, 2021). In that sense, McIntyre and Abrams argued, 'Fraser's "participatory parity" lens allows us to consider how far systemic factors affect the ways in which schools and those within them respond to the needs of young new arrivals' (2021, p. 31).

This argument further reinforces the idea that the resumption of ordinariness, contextualised within a wider framework of social justice as parity-of-participation (Fraser, 2008; 2019; see full details in Chapter 2), is critical for understanding the educational experiences of young Syrian refugees in England (and Lebanon). When refugee children are equally recognised as fellow humans and peers in daily school interactions, when they are allocated the necessary resources to participate on a par with their peers, and when their opinions are heard and their needs (feeling safe, growing webs of belonging and tasting success) acted upon, a sense of home can then be regained (see Figure 5.2).

Fraser's framework may also help educators consider the full range of social and political environments, both within and outside of schools, with which these young people are interacting daily. The normative core of Fraser's tripartite framework, the idea that 'justice requires social arrangements that permit all (adult) members of society to interact with one another as peers' (2001, p. 29), provides an objective benchmark against which different claims of injustice can be decided and remedied through school systems. Indeed, 'the response to asylum-seeking and refugee youth provides one of the greatest tests of social justice for any educational system' (Pinson et al., 2010, p. 248).

Figure 5.2 Safety, belonging and success through education. Source: Adapted from McIntyre and Abrams (2021).

The Syrian children's testimonies: Experiencing social justice as a Syrian refugee in an English school

Unlike in the MAPs schools (see Chapters 4 and 7), where there was a strong emphasis on schooling promoting the future success of the children, in the English school the Syrian children highlighted a less positive, backward-looking aspect to their experiences. They repeatedly stressed the insufficient attention given by their London school to their lives as displaced teenage students. This sense of neglect fed into their beliefs that reaching a safe country did not automatically amount to finding a 'home' or a sense of belonging. Hence, most of them expressed their disappointment at what they perceived as a prevailing tendency in their school to, almost exclusively, identify them as traumatised victims of war and displacement. This consequently limited their representation of themselves to displaying only the stories of their journeys at Refugee Day events; rather than recognising the ongoing current dilemmas and challenges they faced as recently-arrived displaced young people. For example, Sultan, a 15-year-old male participant, explained that hardships do not end once young refugees set foot in the country of possible settlement but, rather, crystallise and become more pressing. He explained:

> ... it was not the journey, it was the fact that we had to live in a completely new environment that [was] traumatising ... when we arrived here, we had some very hard times ... we were in a very bad situation for three years ... we were alone with no friends or relatives to lend help ... or support us ... [even] the simplest thing like communicating with people was hard ... because when they spoke, it seemed like they were speaking very, very fast and I didn't understand anything.

Sultan's views echoed most of his friends' perceptions, which elucidated Kohli's (2014) argument that young refugees' journeys cannot merely be confined to the category of the search for physical safety in a new country. These young people have to embark on yet another form of journey once in the country of settlement, in search of a 'sense of home', a belongingness (Kohli, 2011, p. 311), which involves seeking to resume a sense of normality after periods of uncertainty and disruption (McIntyre & Abrams, 2021) and subsequently enjoying the possibility of success. The particular young Syrians in our study attributed their negative experiences of attempting to regain a sense of home and being able and willing to learn in and through their school to:

a) the misrecognition (or the complete non-recognition) of who they are and their needs, circumstances and daily struggles;
b) the absence of material and moral support to address their issues;
c) and the misrepresentation of who they are and what they really want from their school.

The following sections present the young Syrians' calls for elements of social justice as paving stones to ameliorating their experiences.

The young people's call for recognition

At the forefront of the discussions, the young people stressed the need for their teachers and school leaders to recognise their equal status relative to other students. Four of the students described the absence of fair status recognition in their relationships with teachers and school leaders, manifested in incidents of othering, discrimination and, sometimes, racism. Such lack of recognition was also experienced in their relations with non-Syrian peers, limiting their social inter-actions to their Syrian counterparts and thereby rendering them isolated rather than part of a more diverse and more inclusive school environment. Omar, a 16-year-old male student, described how he rarely felt as though he were 'a human being like everyone else' in the school or that he had equal merit to live a dignified life without being labelled 'a refugee' and considered 'violent' because of 'war trauma'. He said:

> [Some] people here [in the school] do not think about the words they use. They say something to you and don't think of how harmful the consequences might be, and how [what they say] can destroy your soul ... They never think you are a human like them ... but they still expect you to learn and succeed.

Omar's understanding and awareness of the need for social justice underpinned his disappointment at the school practices that shaped his social and educational experience. To him, social justice meant being recognised as a 'boy like all other boys in school' but with a set of adverse prior experiences that yielded specific needs. He often discussed how these needs were overlooked, neglected or met with anger and dismissal, leading him to think that many of his teachers and the school in general 'did not really want to help'; rather, his perception was that they had to accommodate him simply to fulfil the British policy requirements but fell short of supporting him to achieve meaningful learning. Additionally, the notion of social justice in Omar's conversation was always associated with being loved, appreciated and cared for. Such an understanding reflects bell hooks' argument (1994; 2000) that love cannot exist without justice, while justice is not possible without practices guided by loving and compassionate pedagogies in schools (Kaukko et al., 2021). Omar claimed:

> I could not find the [slightest trace] of compassion, care … justice, equality, or help for learning [in this school].

Omar's insights into the need for love also guided his notion of a good teacher:

> A good teacher loves [their] students and respects them. [They] make them feel loved … If I were a teacher, I would make an effort to help my students, I would never hurt … or punish them … I would include them and … make them feel welcomed … I only learn well if I feel accepted and appreciated.

This extract portrays Omar's need to be included and perceived as an equal 'human with feelings and needs' (his words).

Sultan, the other male student in the London study, voiced a similar perspective that linked equality to respect. To him, respect was another form of affection in the classroom that combined being both compassionate and fair to students. Equality must then be enacted through mutual respect between the students and their teachers. In one interview, he explained:

> You cannot find any signs of real respect for students. Most teachers are obligated, perhaps legally, to pretend they respect us … 'oh we respect refugees … oh we believe in equal rights'. That's not true … In return, most students do not respect the teachers.

Sultan perceived that, in this formal school setting, his learning was being undermined as it was impacted by what he conceptualised as the school's 'intended or unintended' *un*familiarity with the learning patterns, needs, and problems of refugee children. In his words:

I love learning, I love to read and think and ponder, but not in this school, not with these teachers who think you will learn [just because] they order you to, rather than help you ... give me a book, give me something that is simple and can help and I promise I will understand ... but maybe they do not care ... [or] do not know how to.

Malak, a 14-year-old female student, spoke of how misrecognising her potential and mistaking her outspoken nature for being a 'bad girl' made her want to 'challenge her teachers' rather than work with them to improve her learning capabilities. She explained:

Never once did they [the teachers] commend my good English ... they see that I achieve well in my exams ... but they keep saying: 'you do not follow the rules' ... They don't like me ... [and] send me out of class if I challenge things or ask questions ... so I miss out on learning and ... they do not seem to care about my learning ... I am like: I will study for my exam just to prove them wrong ... it worries me because this is not genuine learning.

In contrast, Huda, a 15-year-old female participant, shared her experiences of being recognised as 'one of the good Syrian students', stipulating that she wanted to try harder and achieve better results in her exams. She said:

My teachers like me ... they say I can learn because I am quiet and dedicated ... They encourage me to work and say that I have good potential ... I was proud of myself and started trying harder ... I've got better grades in my exams since then because I don't want to disappoint my teachers.

The need for redistribution of resources

Resource redistribution, in the eyes of the six London-based students, was not merely confined to material resources but also included affective issues. Such a perception was portrayed through the children's understanding of the use of power against, rather than in favour of, meeting their needs. As Omar illustrated:

Although we need money to address our many needs ... money is not everything ... the money [allocated] to us through school must go to explaining to teachers that we need help and compassion, not constant threatening ... or silly Refugee Day celebrations.

Malak understood maldistribution as the insufficiency of financial resources that could encourage teachers to strive harder to understand and help their students. She said:

Teachers are changing constantly ... We usually have many substitute teachers and it is hard to believe that they care for us or our needs ... they come here for one day sometimes ... sit down, get their money and leave ... Many teachers only care about being paid ... I don't blame them, they have their families and everything ... but maybe if they were being given more, I mean money and everything, they would care more ... maybe they would see us [Syrians for who we are] ... as children who need to be heard and helped.

Sultan also argued that Syrian children were made to feel a burden and often, unfairly, treated with coercion. He urged that power and more resources should be invested in helping the Syrian students – rather than coercing them. He explained:

Any money given by the government should go to teaching teachers how to help us ... [alas], in this school, headteachers and teachers think that holding power over the students can solve all [problems] ... 'We have the power to kick you out of school!' Do you know how many times we have heard the vice-principal say that? ... You don't want us? ... Then why do you have us here? Why don't you help us and support our needs ... before judging and hoping to kick us out?

Relatedly, Sultan discussed how his understanding of social justice was shaped by his perceptions of power and its relationship to economic positioning. Moreover, in an authoritarian institution (as he perceived his school to be), social justice could not exist because power relationships were unequal. He recounted:

I sometimes dream that I am ruling the world and cancelling the authority of [power and] money over people – a world where everything is for free; and teachers teach ... for the goodness of the act and for the peace of the world.

The children's perceptions regarding resources and fairness reflected two very important points. The first stressed their opinions on the impact of maldistribution of resources within their school, which was associated with teachers needing training about more just pedagogies that could accommodate children's needs. The second point concerned power dynamics in school, where the threat of being excluded from lessons and/or from school was always looming, inhibiting affective and compassionate support. This also fed into refugee children feeling denied the resources to become equal partners, since they were being treated as a burden to be tackled. In addition, what the students were calling for amounts to, in our terms of reference, adequate, affective and compassionate pedagogies that would cater to their needs and help promote their participation and learning. Further, they acknowledged that such pedagogies required adequate distribution of available resources that would enable teachers to better foster inclusion and equality and teach, in Sultan's words, '[for] the goodness of the act'.

The requirement for representation

The children's perceived absence of access to representation further reinforced their sense of powerlessness and led them to believe that relationships built on coercion were prerequisites to their participation and success. Malak extended this idea, connecting it to the tendency of teachers to ignore students' opinions and problems, which, in her view, made the school appear ignorant of the refugee children's needs and uncaring toward their concerns. She said:

> School [and] teachers could have been a [buffer] against what we face every day in and out of school … but teachers never listen and do not care to ask what's wrong or whether we need help … They never asked whether I was coping … learning … or what issues I had … All that matters [to them] is following the rules.

Huda also described how, for refugee children, compliance with the rules was a *condition* for being treated well. Huda found that arguing for her needs would only cause further exclusion, while her peers believed that arguing could lead to benefits. She spoke of knowing the key to building good relationships with teachers, which was to prove to them that she was well-behaved and wanted to stay out of trouble by sitting alone and away from other 'Syrian and Arab students' in class, and by being obedient and polite to staff. In this framing, Huda clearly connected success with conformity, as follows:

> Teachers here are always angry and stressed, but if you know how to be nice and polite to them … show them that you are not like the other Syrian students who are perceived as troublesome … concentrate on doing your work … [and] follow instructions without arguing … teachers will like you.

However, these perceptions of subordination seemed to impair children's feelings of safety and belonging, as expressed as follows, by Omar:

> At first, I was not given a chance to belong here, but now … due to all these issues, I do not want to belong … I have become indifferent, and after I cried too much, I have no tears left and I do not know what to do to feel accepted.

Sultan also associated the lack of representation with a lack of a sense of belonging and willingness to learn:

> I just know I don't belong here and now there is this voice inside me that says 'you should not be here, school will not get you anywhere, you can do better than that because school is silencing you and limiting your abilities' … What will happen if I fail again and again? I don't want to feel like a loser because school decided I cannot do this or that … they don't hear me … [but] I want to be an achiever … I want to find a place where I can feel heard … [and be] successful and content.

Parity-of-participation and regaining a sense of home

The foregoing testimonies spoke to the Syrian students' perceptions of their inability to participate on equal terms with other children in their everyday school lives. They felt unheard, unappreciated and only conditionally included, which impacted negatively on their feelings of safety, belonging and willingness to learn. They described how these expressions of marginalisation underpinned their struggles to adapt and make themselves at home in their new resettlement context. Sultan expressed these feelings as follows:

I am always reminded that I should be grateful that I was given the chance to come here … and that we act as if we are entitled to be here … It is not like I think it's my right to be here … but I might actually have it as a right because this earth does not belong to anyone … [and] we are all equal … they don't help much when they say, 'if you don't like it here then go back to your country' … A teacher once said: 'You Syrians are aggressive … why do you bring your war problems to school?' … Living does not automatically mean someone belongs. Even if you feel that you belong, you do not become fully English … [especially] when you are reminded every day that you are not … we have heard many saying, 'Why are you coming to our country? You are stealing our money!'

Omar illustrated where his sense of belonging was still placed:

I belong with all my heart and soul to Syria and my Arabic origins … Even if I ever got British nationality, I would always remain Syrian and seek to be among my people … [as] they accept me for who I am … [as opposed to] labelling me as traumatised and violent without asking or helping me … we do not feel that we belong to this country.

Huda's experience, in contrast, affirms a positive connection between the presence of some conditions of social justice as parity-of-participation and her will to make the resettlement country her home:

Here [in Britain], women feel valued and know that they have rights … unlike [my town in] Syria … We were never taught respect in such a way; especially when it comes to respecting and valuing women … I might not be a fully-fledged British person yet, but I do want to be … I feel that I belong to this country and that I am already a part of it … Britain to me now is similar to how Syria once felt, and I would never leave it … because this country teaches you that women are equal to men.

Reflections on testimonies of displaced young people in the London school

The aim of this study was to explore, through a lens of social justice, how Syrian refugee children who settled permanently in London experienced learning and navigated daily social interactions at school. It also sought to examine how all these experiences shaped the process of bringing a sense of ordinariness to this new and unfamiliar home. This study recognises that Syrian displaced children have always owned their own voices, perceptions and opinions; but these, as they perceived, may have been muted, unexpressed, neglected or taken for granted. Therefore, the research aimed to provide a platform for the young Syrians to express their thoughts and reflect on their new lives as refugee children in a culturally different setting where they were required to learn and communicate in a new language and adapt to new social norms. This vivid and longitudinal representation of the Syrian children's experiences not only highlights the principles of social justice but also provides teachers, practitioners and policymakers with valuable insights into the lives and experiences of displaced Syrian children in a permanent post-settlement context (in contrast to the MAPs children in Lebanon, whose setting remained officially 'temporary').

As expressed in the overall theoretical framing of this book, for refugee children in a resettlement context, regaining a sense of ordinariness and a sense of home requires the enjoyment of safety, which paves the way toward forming circles of belonging and developing a will to learn, prosper and succeed (Kohli, 2011). However, this will only be the case if and when Fraser's (2008) conditions of social justice – that permit participation on a par with others in the host society – are fulfilled (McIntyre & Abrams, 2021). As illustrated by the children's own views displayed in this chapter, the feeling of safety attached to having the legal right to stay in the UK was not enough to promote a sense of belonging. Instead, the young Syrians expressed how, in the absence of feeling socially safe – specifically, by being loved, respected and actively included in their everyday schooling experiences – they experienced feelings of exclusion and non-belonging. In turn, their will to learn and succeed in school was hampered.

These testimonies and reflections from the children resonate well with Kaukko et al.'s argument (2021, pp. 3–4) that feeling safe and being able to belong in educational settings requires 'pedagogies of love' to be employed. These authors stipulate that, for refugee children to feel safe and included in their school environment, teachers and school leaders need to establish the following:

> … personal connections and faith in human potential [that] are at the heart of pedagogical encounters, [whereby] love in such

pedagogy is composed of care, commitment, responsibility, respect, trust, and knowledge … This love is political, public and relational; it is not transgressive, private, or physical. It is more than an emotion tied to the private sphere and home.

The concept of pedagogies of love entails creating and sustaining reciprocal arrangements that cultivate caring practices in educational settings for school leaders, teachers and children. This requires considering the wellbeing and needs of both children and educators, which begins by establishing connections and relationships of trust and respect between teachers and children, leaders and teachers, and leaders and children. It is both political and critical in its aim to empower children and educators while creating safe, inclusive and caring educational environments where children's needs are met, belonging is optimised and learning can ensue, as called for by the Syrian children in this book. 'Adding more love' to education, as one of our pupils in Lebanon expressed it, is not a fleeting expression of personal feelings, nor is it a momentary act of empathy toward only *some* pupils. Rather, it requires a committed and sustained effort to continually build a caring community in educational institutions, particularly those hosting refugee, displaced or disadvantaged children.

The children's testimonies also revealed their understanding of the need to have social justice measures in place to support feelings of safety, foster belonging and encourage success. That is why most of them argued that the absence of recognition and representation in their daily schooling interactions was detrimental to their will to learn and succeed. Unlike the experiences of the MAPs children presented in Chapter 4, the Syrian children in the London study believed that their humanity and previous educational experiences, capital, capacities, talents, needs and voices were not recognised or valued but ignored. Such feelings contributed to further alienation from the educational and social environment of the school and inhibited their efforts to succeed in traditional ways or develop new skills and talents. As Sultan explained, school was 'killing their ambitions'.

The children were also aware of their right to representation and the power dynamics in their school that they perceived to be muting their self-expression and suppressing their articulation of their educational needs (where raising one's voice was considered disobedience). These power dynamics were also seen to be connected to the notion of maldistribution, whereby the Syrian children believed that those in institutionally strategic positions exercised coercion to solve problems instead of allocating adequate resources and measures to recognise and act on the needs of the refugee children.

Finally, the call for teachers to be compassionate and loving, according to the young Syrians, was connected closely to feeling safe but also fundamentally entrenched in a wider understanding of socially just relations that would enable them to develop a sense of belonging and a taste of real success. The implications of the perceived negative connotations of their relationship with school and teachers impacted on the children's will to learn or achieve. Their perceptions of being a burden to their teachers and the school were at odds with being able to achieve meaningful learning, and this exacerbated their feeling of not belonging in the school. Throughout the journeys tracked by this study, the children repeatedly expressed a plea to their teachers to adopt socially-just practices to help them feel included rather than alienated, appreciated rather than rejected, and in receipt of support and help to learn rather than being treated as a burden. The representations in this case study can thus raise awareness among teachers responsible for refugee children that school has the potential to be a sanctuary and home away from home.

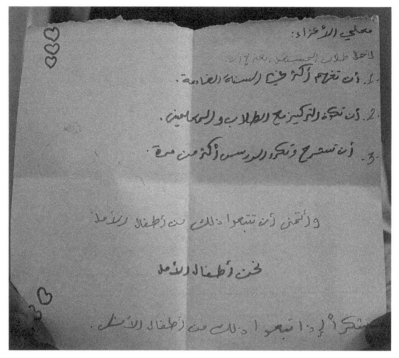

Figure 6.1 A MAPs pupil's letter to their teacher. © The authors.

My dear teachers,

For the future students, we suggest to you that:

1- You'd make us understand the lessons more next year
2- You concentrate and follow up with the students and [other] teachers
3- You'd explain and repeat the lesson more than once.

Thank you for following this advice from Children of Hope

6
Fighting to keep Syrian refugee children in North Lebanon learning during school closures: Case study 3

The research activities for Chapters 4 and 5 took place just prior to the COVID-19 pandemic that interrupted schooling around the world. In Lebanon, 1.2 million children missed out on two years of formal education when schools closed because of the political uprisings during October, November and December 2019, followed by the pandemic (2019–20 and 2020–1). The economic collapse that occurred simultaneously resulted in families struggling to meet basic needs, which consequently increased the risk of children not returning to education once schools reopened because they either accepted paid labour or early marriage instead (Save the Children, 2021; UNICEF et al., 2021).

At the end of these two exceptional academic years, children in Lebanese schools were promoted by default to the next grade level, regardless of their academic progress. This was a break with the convention in Lebanon that children needed to pass a series of threshold-level assessments at the end of each school year to gain access to the next grade. With automatic promotion, children not only missed certain foundational concepts in their learning but also the socialisation that they normally engaged in during break times in the playground or, less frequently, in the classroom. It is through social interactions at school or other education settings that children tend to achieve their sense of belonging, learn to manage emotions and develop concepts of self. Hence, the prolonged absence of lessons and socialisation due to school closures in Lebanon undermined opportunities for children who were already vulnerable to marginalisation to strengthen foundations of knowledge, wellbeing and social and emotional growth. The resulting vacuum in these refugee children's developmental journeys thus significantly impairs their opportunities to participate fairly and equally with others.

This chapter captures testimonies from Lebanese and Syrian teachers who endeavoured to support Syrian refugee children during school closures in North Lebanon, one of the most economically vulnerable governorates in the country. On several occasions in 2021, we visited teachers and children at Relief & Reconciliation for Syria (RRS), an NGO in the North Lebanon governorate that provides NFE programmes for Syrian refugee children. In many ways, RRS is a very different NGO from MAPs. At RRS, while over three-quarters of the teachers are themselves Syrian refugees, the rest are Lebanese. Some of the Lebanese teachers also work in second-shift provision within state schools. The RRS classrooms have only a few Lebanese children from the local host community, the majority of children being Syrian refugees, some of whom are in the second-shift in state schools and attend the NFE programmes at RRS for additional support.

During the four visits we undertook to this NGO (from May to June 2021), teachers shared their experiences and reflections with us through focus group discussions. We also had the opportunity to observe classes in action (see Figure 6.2). The testimonials and observations reveal what kind of education is made available to this population of Syrian refugee children and how it is delivered. They not only demonstrate just how limited the spaces for children to share their visions and reflections of

Figure 6.2   Typical example of an RRS classroom, North Lebanon.
Photo © Bassel Akar.

learning are but also reveal context-specific threats to the availability of quality education to Syrian refugee children in Lebanon. What we learn from their contributions and our observations can help inform approaches to level the field of participation for Syrian-refugee and host-community Lebanese children vulnerable to crises.

Starting from zero

As the second year of school closure neared its end, teachers across Lebanon painted a grim picture when talking about children's learning status. They expressed a great deal of concern when explaining how children had missed so much learning time in school, and felt that they needed to start 'from zero' – an expression most teachers used. They observed how these children had either no, or a weak, foundation to whatever discipline they were learning. This included language, the arts, maths and sciences. Illustrating the consequence of such a long period of enforced absence, one teacher observed that, 'Children in Grades 2 and 3 do not have the basics in language; so, we're starting from zero'. The grade-level promotions during the two years of lockdown meant that children who had only previously been to kindergarten suddenly now reappeared in Grade 2. Even many of those in Grade 3 'still [did] not know the letters', according to one teacher. Another argued that a further cause of lost learning was the 'overemphasis on psychosocial support' prior to school closures. This view illustrates a rather dominant pedagogical attitude among teachers and caregivers that emphasises academic attainment as the primary – if not sole – purpose of schooling, at the expense of other essential outcomes.

The lost learning opportunities appeared to have cornered these teachers on the remedial NFE programme into a dilemma: 'Do we just continue with the grade-appropriate curriculum material? Or should we be going back to the child-appropriate foundational basics that the children are missing?' This dilemma manifests in different ways, including in the matter of homework. The children send their homework to these support teachers for help via WhatsApp. For example, as their science subjects are taught in French and 'the children do not have a base in French', some teachers invest time in teaching the language to support the children in their science lessons. However, one teacher explained that choosing between concepts missed (such as language) or regular homework was not feasible and, therefore, they tried to 'balance between the two'. Even the children in secondary schools were struggling. One Grade 12 teacher commented that her pupils' English/French language proficiency remained at the Grade 6 level, with only a quarter of the children 'proficient enough to study science and math in the second language'.

The classrooms: Online and in-person

The teachers shared their struggles and innovative approaches to supporting the refugee children whose families had, in most cases, very limited online connectivity and access to only one mobile phone for the whole family. This was typically shared with siblings but taken by the father (or main household salary earner) to work. Each of the NFE teachers created a WhatsApp group using the parents' phone numbers, to which the children would send audio and video recordings that their schoolteachers (in the state schools) had prepared, because they did not understand the instructions or the material being covered. Sometimes, even the NFE teachers had to take time to understand the lesson or instructions because, as one explained: 'The [schoolteachers'] WhatsApp messages are not clear; sometimes they have so much background noise of neighbours playing and children shouting at home.' The NFE teachers would then prepare simplified instructions in 10–15-minute audio recordings.

Sometimes, they added images showing how to solve the problem or approach the task. Often, this interaction via WhatsApp meant that some of these support teachers drew on knowledge or concepts outside the Lebanese National Curriculum. One Lebanese teacher (who teaches at the NFE programme and at a local public school) asserted: 'I'm using my own resources; if the inspector wants to challenge me, I'll take him to the Ministry. It's the books. They all need to be thrown into the garbage.' The teachers on the NFE programme claimed they often ended up communicating individually with children and parents, as late as 11 pm or even midnight. Other challenges they reported included that some children who were able to connect for online support kept their cameras off and did not participate.

Some breakthroughs that teachers seemed proud to share, however, included the friendships they had ended up creating with the children through the individual communication. They felt that these children engaged more during the support sessions and showed more commitment to learning the material as a result of the mobile phone liaison. Some teachers said they created connections with the children when using materials with which the children were familiar. The maths teacher, for example, said that using marbles to teach number placements appeared to have motivated the children's interest. A Lebanese state-school teacher who was also part of the NFE team reported devoting one hour a week to 'talk[ing] about non-academic things, anything'.

These testimonials demonstrate the very limited space within online modalities for encouraging children to openly express their ideas and views. However, they also show that using online platforms for individual support can still provide a safe and engaging space for children and their parents, including when conversations do not relate directly to learning literacy and numeracy.

Wellbeing of children and teachers

The recent successive crises, including lockdown, the devaluation of the local currency and the destruction caused by the port explosion have taken an emotional toll on virtually the entire population in Lebanon. Even prior to COVID-19, teachers and caregivers faced varying degrees of burnout and other forms of emotional fatigue (Chinnery & Akar, 2021). Teachers – whether Lebanese or Syrian and regardless of teaching in the second-shift, NFE or day-shift state schools – have faced traumatic daily struggles to secure basic living needs (such as food, electricity or money) while still remaining committed to their pupils' learning. Clearly, as all teachers explained, the salaries in Lebanese Pounds after the currency crash could no longer keep up with the soaring cost of living. One teacher explained that sometimes they taught from the car to keep their phone charged and ensure a suitably quiet environment for online classes. The teachers reminded us that many of the state schools went on strike to protest against low salaries.

Teachers reported how children's participation in learning activities was being stymied by an emotional state of mind shaped by school closures and hard-to-access online learning, in addition to instabilities at home, including poor living conditions and domestic violence. The teachers we spoke with found that their pupils felt 'neglected', 'disposable' and helpless at their school and, consequently, 'over-dependent' on any opportunity for support.

They also shared observations of how children relied heavily on teachers' empathy to excuse them from not doing the work asked of them, and on caregivers doing the homework with or for them. Furthermore, most of the children in the final year of secondary school were reportedly not studying because they were gambling on the chances that the MEHE would issue another blanket promotion as it had done the previous year when the official exams were cancelled.

Children's feelings of abandonment and varying degrees of over-dependence did not emerge only during school closures. We hypothesise in this chapter, based on our interviews and observations, that schooling prior to the compounded crises, coupled with difficult home living environments, had socialised the children into individuals who needed to passively follow instructions and retain knowledge to please the teacher or parent. Nevertheless, children's dependency on teachers and caregivers for academic achievement and wellbeing apparently surfaced more than ever during the subsequent period.

The teachers at this NGO also observed their pupils feeling stressed when 'someone raises their voice' because they associated anger with the corporal punishment they experienced at home. Hence, children coming from homes riddled with violence and neglect were likely to exercise greater degrees of caution and self-critique, as we witnessed with a few of the children with whom we worked. Some were afraid of disappointing or upsetting adults with the ideas they wrote and shared. One of the older-age girls ripped up her paper after drafting a letter to her teacher and cried (and, fortunately, we were able to show sensitivity to her position and comfort her without drawing too much attention from her peers). Teachers also associated violence at home with children's approaches to play and managing conflicts with friends. Although the children appeared to engage in friendly play, a football coach explained that many 'lose their temper' by abandoning the activity, shouting or hitting out during games or practice.

Pedagogies of knowledge transmission and retention

Observing the NFE classrooms revealed legacies of a culture of learning and teaching directed toward the retention of knowledge through repetition. This pedagogy was strongly reflected in the language of learning used when teachers asked children to *sammi'* (recite) and *ihfaz* (memorise). The children were asked to repeatedly write letters in rows and read the same sentences over and over again. When reading aloud, the children were apparently expected to follow a certain pace; when one child paused briefly to decipher a difficult word, the teacher jumped in and read instead. During language classes, such as French, verbal drilling emerged as a core practice. In another exercise, the teacher pointed to each word, reading it aloud and asking the children to repeat it, informing them, 'You'll recite it to me later'. In another language class, she asked the children to 'go home and repeat this many times out loud so that you can hear yourself, memorise and recite to your teacher at school'.

The classroom observations also picked up an affective dimension that reflected frustration among the teachers toward both noise and how long the children often took to read something or solve a problem. The limited tolerance of noise was expressed mostly by Lebanese teachers when they would exhort, 'be quiet!', 'sshhh', 'hurry!' and 'stop talking!' In one class, a boy was crying and a support teacher soon became frustrated and kept asking him to either stop or go home. Finally, she said to his sister (who was also in the class): 'I'm going to tell your mum not to bring him here anymore.' Teachers also appeared to become irritated very quickly when children took time to learn a particular point or carry out exercises in class. After teachers posed a question, they gave the children just one or two seconds to respond. Unwilling to wait any longer, they would hastily answer it themselves. Sometimes, they raised their voices and snapped at the children, 'we've been doing this for a while!' and 'come on, focus!'

Facilitating equal opportunities for participation, in the case of these children, requires those who missed out on learning opportunities during school closures to receive remedial support to ensure a degree of mastery in the core concepts expected at approximately their stage of child development. The cost of the closures appears to include tensions between the children's NFE teachers and those from state schools, as the former endeavour to prioritise a return to the foundations that have been missed or insufficiently covered, while schoolteachers seek to adhere to the current stage of the National Curriculum. Moreover, NFE teachers' attempts to coordinate efforts with parents and children to help the latter 'catch up' eat into their personal time. This going above and beyond the time scheduled for non-formal schooling takes its toll on the teachers' emotional wellbeing and, most likely, that of parents and children as well. Threats to children's parity-of-participation are also present at home, where younger children are more vulnerable to marginalisation and limited access to digital tools for distance learning. Clearly, for better or for worse, the roles, integrity and resources of parents and teachers determine the children's experiences, which will either sustain fair and equitable learning and socialisation opportunities or undermine them.

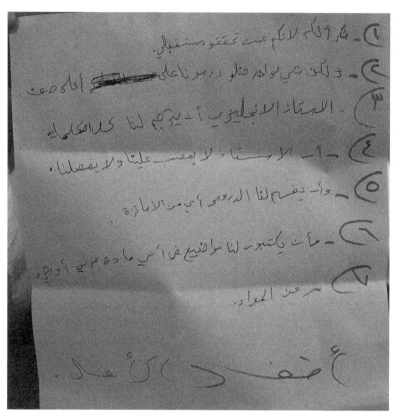

Figure 7.1 A MAPs pupil's letter to their teacher. © The authors.

Dear Teachers

Thank you for helping me have a future!
One thing though, please keep on teaching us all the way through to the highest
grade …
Our teacher would never be angry with us, nor exclude us from the school.
All teachers explain the lessons very well to us.

Child of Hope

7

Refugee children's experiences during closures, crises and COVID

This chapter continues the focus from Chapter 4 on children attending non-formal primary provision in learning centres run by MAPs in the Beqaa Valley, Lebanon. It narrates how teachers have drawn on the children's representations presented in the original research workshops to improve their learning, relationships and aspirations during and after the COVID-19 pandemic that closed schools in 2020.

Compounded crises

Shortly after the workshop sessions described in Chapter 4 had ended, a series of national crises began to layer in 2019, which have had a significant impact on the continuity of learning for the children with whom we had been working and, indeed, for children across all communities in Lebanon. Political uprisings in the country involving thousands of people began on 17 October 2019, in protest at government corruption. The ensuing tensions and uncertainty accelerated the export of US dollars that had begun prior to the uprisings. Consequently, the Lebanese Pound started to crash in terms of its 'street' value, as opposed to the official rate at which the authorities had pegged the currency; and, by April 2022, the LBP had lost around 90 per cent of its value (European Parliament, 2022). With government subsidies for petrol and medicine, a black market emerged, causing shortages in essential resources to cover basic needs, including fuel for transportation and electricity, food and medicine.

The economic collapse was further exacerbated by the massive explosion that devastated the port of Beirut on 4 August 2020, the result

of a combination of factors including negligible management accountability and poor safety measures that saw a warehouse of highly explosive
material left unmonitored (BBC, 2020). In addition to the fatalities, the
explosion displaced nearly 300,000 Beirut residents and caused damage
to 163 schools (UNESCO, 2020).

The fall-out from this tragedy, combined with Lebanon's unfolding
economic collapse, pushed more than half the country's population
below the poverty line (World Bank, 2021) and triggered a series of
crippling actions involving the closure of public services, including
schools. Additionally, many roads were blocked by protestors, which
limited the ability of teachers to get to school sites, even when there
were no officially enforced closures. This was the case for the nine
MAPs education centres described earlier in this book. Then, in a further
layer of adversity, the COVID-19 pandemic began to take hold in the
region, forcing the closure of all education institutions in Lebanon.
These compounded crises pushed thousands of Lebanese families out
of low-cost private schools, or out of schooling altogether, and led to a
systemic shutdown of the second-shift state schooling for Syrian refugee
children (Chinnery & Akar, 2021). These disruptions to learning were,
of course, in addition to the disruption already inflicted on the Syrian
children by the war in their homeland, from which they had initially fled.

These multiple, compounded crises brought these children another
level of instability and harm. In this chapter, we draw on our own observations as well as further testimonies and reflections on how the children
were affected. We illustrate the state of affairs in education and daily life
that further distanced these young refugees from parity-of-participation
and success.

The Syrian refugee children at MAPs during the COVID-19 pandemic

In common with all education settings in Lebanon, the MAPs learning
centres were forced to close due to the COVID-19 pandemic, from March
2020. For the MAPs children, however, the COVID restrictions were
less 'impromptu' and more enduring than the local disruptions related
to the economy and civil unrest had been. Just like education providers
globally, MAPs had to rethink their models of learning and teaching
during this time. The organisation's core team quickly decided that the
most efficient way to continue to facilitate learning was through the
establishment of classes via WhatsApp, using parents' mobile phones and

contact numbers. WhatsApp was regarded as the most accessible digital platform, being available on the widest range of devices and minimising the amount of data used. This is consistent with the pattern of device availability noted in a study of Syrian children during COVID lockdowns in Jordan, Turkey and Lebanon (Abu Moghli & Shuayb, 2020).

Children would therefore study at home, usually in their temporarily constructed shelters, as best they could. In a small number of cases, especially later in the lockdown period, it was possible to provide limited photocopied resources where families had no access to phones or adequate data. The distribution of these resources was greatly aided by the fact that MAPs' logistics staff were already accessing the camps as part of its health programmes. In this sense, the distribution of educational resources was given some support.

As a research team, we were able to return in-person to the MAPs education centres midway through 2021, not long after the children had returned to in-person learning. We observed class sessions and had informal conversations with staff and children. We were also fortunate to have the opportunity to undertake more formal discussions with some of the children who had just completed their primary schooling and were anywhere between 11 and 15 years old at this point. This age range was accounted for by the periods of schooling missed due to the children's displacement (see Chapter 4).

Our discussions, which included their experiences of learning during the COVID-19 pandemic, took the form of small, informal focus-group sessions as well as paired interviews; all these sessions were semi-structured in nature and were conducted in two of the MAPs schools. These research activities formed part of Brian Lally's wider doctoral study, which was conducted as a 'life-histories' project exploring the educational and life experiences of Syrian children seeking refuge in Lebanon. The study received favourable ethical reviews in both the UK and Lebanon. A Syrian Arabic translator was present throughout all the sessions, although the children sometimes spoke in English. The sessions were transcribed by Brian Lally, and translations were reviewed at that point as a reliability measure.

Challenges during remote learning

The children at the MAPs schools, like most children in Lebanon, had restricted access to mobile devices and data to continue their learning. The limited availability of digital technology and the inability to purchase or access it were clear examples of poor distribution of material resources among the children. Indeed, maldistribution largely determined the extent to which they had a fair chance to participate (Fraser, 2008; 2019). This was due not only to the limited number of devices – almost always only one per family – and data costs but also to the number of school-aged siblings they had, who would all potentially require access to the same device throughout the day.

Unsurprisingly, the children reported the negative consequences within family dynamics of competition over accessing the highly restricted devices (and, therefore, competition over access to learning). As one of the girls explained:

> I had my two sisters and two brothers studying with me, so we fought because we only had one working phone in the house. A lot of fights happened because of the phone.

The children reported finding it very hard to concentrate on their learning while at home. They live in small, makeshift shelters with only two or three small rooms that they share with their parents and their (sometimes numerous) siblings – see our accompanying film (UCL Institute of Education, 2021) for footage. One student shared a reflection that was typical among others:

> We didn't understand, when we were studying online. When we attended the school, we understood the lessons better. The teacher was on the video and we would [be] on the video; it's a very difficult thing … We were sitting with all the family, so someone would speak or someone would scream … Because when … all the family is sitting beside me, and my sister and brothers, and they are speaking … I can't focus [on] the lessons. And the phones, we only have one phone [shared between us all]; and the battery is always empty and the internet [connection] is bad. And there's my sisters and brothers, they have different lessons, me and them, but the lessons [are at] the same time …

In contrast, some children were nevertheless expressive of how they were helping and supporting each other to participate in school learning during this time. As one boy appreciatively observed: 'We were helping each other. Me and her [his sister] were on the same phone.' To which his sister responded, 'For example, if there is a question and I don't understand it, he will help me with it.'

Some families made arrangements for their children to work with neighbours who had children in the same classes. MAPs also tried to facilitate greater participation by allocating time slots to different grades where the teachers of those classes would be online. The children expressed appreciation of these efforts to address the maldistribution of resources that undermined their participation. Indeed, the children linked the teachers' efforts to continue teaching them to a sense that their teachers really cared about them, while telling of awareness among their friends and relatives that teachers in other schools were not going to such lengths to be supportive. One child said: 'If it was someone else [another school], they wouldn't teach us. It is good that they cared about us and taught us.' Such efforts serve as a concrete example of staff trying to intervene directly to restore status equality, at least to the level the children would have previously enjoyed through their in-person engagement with schooling. This afforded them a taste of justice through recognition, enabled via interaction with their peers and teachers.

Overwhelmingly, however, MAPs pupils' experiences of attempting to learn from home during the pandemic were negative. As one put it, in a direct but telling understatement: 'It's hard.' Besides their inability to access materials online, the most common concern the children expressed was the difficulties they faced in grasping what the teacher was trying to convey, and frustration at knowing that these difficulties were not so acute with in-person learning experiences 'because the lessons in the online, we didn't … understand the teaching', whereas '[i]f the teacher is in front of you, she will explain it for you'. The children really missed the opportunity to ask questions, whether during or outside the scheduled sessions, and to check their understanding with their teachers, as well as missing their physical presence. As some of them explained:

> We don't have the luxury of asking the teacher; for example, if we have a question, we don't have time to ask.
> We [have to] text online while the lesson is going on. A lot of students ask, so the question is buried in the chat and the teacher doesn't see it.

The children seemed aware of missing their expected opportunities to participate in learning during the period of remote study. They were therefore not so much resigned to having to go over lessons again when they were finally able to return to the classroom but, rather, welcoming of the opportunity to do so. However, they did find this process arduous, recognising that they needed to feel better prepared for their final exams.

One explained that they felt anxious 'because there were many lessons that we didn't understand, so we came to repeat them ... and there was a short period of time to the exam'. As a result of returning to class and repeating the learning, one child claimed:

> I understand it more than before because, before, there might be something that I missed or I didn't know how to do. There would be something that the teacher repeated, and when the teacher asks about it [in class, upon returning to in-person learning], I would want to answer it.

The children expressed their commitment to working hard in the resumed in-person sessions to catch up on what they had missed and were ready to show the teachers that they were doing so. They also showed an awareness of how the disruption to their learning might further exacerbate their disadvantaged position among the globe's children as their school learning became even more reduced – an illustration of injustice.

The desire they expressed to do well and please the teacher by doing so was part of a general sense of great relief, happiness and excitement at being in the company of teachers and friends once again. These encouraging expressions are likely to have stemmed from the children's deep attachment to their teachers and the sense of safety and belonging they felt in their MAPs school community. These feelings are entirely consistent with the fulfilment of needs identified by Kohli (2011) as critical for displaced children. Quite simply, as one of the young learners put it during interview, she was 'so happy and excited' to return to school; and another echoed this sentiment, saying: 'It was so beautiful. It was so beautiful that I saw the teachers and my friends.' This same student was equally clear in her summary of the challenges she had faced during remote learning and of the value she placed in discussing her learning with her peers after returning to face-to-face instruction: '[A]t home, there is noise. You can't focus on the teacher. [But, when we were in school,] the students were talking with each other, talking after the class [about learning].'

In a sense, compared to many other displaced Syrian children in Lebanon, these children were fortunate to have received any form of provision at all, even though that provision might have been limited and problematic. It is telling that the children were aware of this too, including from their contacts with friends and relatives in Lebanon and in other countries, again suggesting their participation in engaging with global issues (see Chapter 4). But their experiences clearly expose the disparity of access to social justice that was routine in their lives, made still more limited under lockdown. And this is exactly in line with the underscored amplification of systemic inequalities caused by the COVID-19 'rupture' to education for Syrian children in Lebanon noted by Menashy and Zakharia (2022).

Education providers have proudly described their efforts to make curricula and materials available online during the pandemic period. However, for huge numbers of already marginalised children around the world, these good intentions have been quite simply irrelevant because of the poor distribution of digital tools as well as the unavailability of power and internet data in many locations where displaced people are hosted (You et al., 2020). At MAPs, we have seen that the staff did manage to send copies of resources tailored to the learning needs of the children, including textbooks or even digital devices to some children. Yet, we asked ourselves, how many of these young people have the emotional or physical space to meaningfully engage with these materials in ways similar to more privileged peers who enjoy quiet, calm locations as well as unrestricted access to learning resources and encouraging parents who actively support their learning? And to what extent are we fostering a holistic education community that directly listens when children tell us about the tensions in their home lives and the demands of family life in resource-deprived contexts, which impact so much on their development and learning? In other words, as a broad community of practice, how fully do educators play their part in ensuring meaningful representation of children as a contributory means to achieving social justice?

Teachers' agency for MAPs children's representations of their experiences

One group of people who were directly able and willing to act on the MAPs children's representations (before, during and after the pandemic) were their teachers, themselves displaced Syrians. Teachers interviewed during the workshops in 2019 were positive in planning to act on what the children had to say, picking out themes, for example, of curriculum expansion and active learning (see Figure 7.2). They were considering the broader lives of the children with whom they worked and their wellbeing as human beings with a right to parity-of-participation. A particularly unexpected response was their view of the shift in the dynamic of the roles in the teacher–pupil relationship, and in the expectations surrounding these roles. This related directly to their perception of the value, importance and potential of opening up opportunities on a regular basis for children to express their ideas and opinions openly to teachers. This was a novel idea to the teachers at the time of our original workshops. One teacher explained in response to the children's representations:

> [They] enlightened me on something that I was not aware of. I might be doing something wrong while teaching without realising it. Everyone makes mistakes and one must improve one's practice. So, just as they accept us and what we do all the time, we should also accept them and take what they say seriously.

Teachers also acknowledged how challenging this representation could be for the children as well as for themselves. But they expressed pride that the children managed to achieve it, nonetheless. A different teacher reflected during an interview in May 2019:

> It was something novel and unfamiliar for a child to express their thoughts to their teacher. It is something they are not used to; it is a new idea … Some of them apologised at the end of the presentation as they thought they had done something bad. No, it was not a bad thing, they just expressed their needs and opinions; this is a positive thing, and we welcome such an approach.

The teachers expressed their understanding not only of the importance of hearing what the children thought about their lessons and activities in their schools but also of how crucial it is to understand more fully the feelings and broader lives of the children in their care. They also recognised that spaces (both literal and figurative) in which such powerful communication can take place may be rare to find in education centres. As one teacher expressed during an interview:

> I was excited to know what they have to tell us, their pain and their agony, because they never speak of that in the classroom, they never tell us how they feel. They only come to learn. We do have this 'life skills' session; they do activities during the session but you cannot know how they feel! … I was ready to listen to what they had to say.

Although these teachers were clearly receptive to the ideas of the children immediately following the workshops in 2019 (as described in

Figure 7.2 'My classroom' by a Syrian refugee pupil at a MAPs education centre. © The authors.

Chapter 4), it is unclear how much the teachers have changed, or been able to change, in their practice since the time of the original research workshops. Restricted capacity for teachers' development of practice was exacerbated by the subsequent school closures and other effects of the COVID-19 pandemic and the economic collapse in Lebanon, as outlined earlier. For example, returning arts and sports to the curriculum has proven to be logistically very challenging for the MAPs administration in a context of dramatically decreasing funds and increasing time pressure to 'catch up' on lost opportunities for learning fundamental concepts in academic subjects.

Two years after the original research, we were able to speak in person with some of the teachers who had participated in the workshops. One of them is now a principal in a MAPs teaching centre. He described how well he remembered two key points the children had represented back at the start: (1) teachers including more activities during lessons to facilitate learning through play and (2) teachers helping the children with the learning process by giving them more time to think about their responses to questions (see Chapter 8 for further discussion of this topic). On the impact of the original research sessions and what he learned from the children at the time, this teacher reflected: 'I think I became better as a teacher. I acquired new strategies and new techniques for these children' (interview, June 2021). This openness to new ideas seems to have been ongoing. He expressed particular delight at one example he gave of some of the kindergarten children (aged 4–5 years) he teaches, who stopped his English lesson to teach him a game to play with them to work more effectively with the flashcards he was using at the time.

Perhaps even more striking, however, was that this teacher (and now school leader) had not only carefully considered the idea of listening to, and acting upon, the ideas of the children in his care but also, through listening, was trying to understand the children more meaningfully. This understanding appeared to drive his determination to provide an environment for the children that would maximise their participation, despite limited resources, and their sense of safety, belonging and success. This educator, himself a Syrian refugee living in hugely challenging circumstances, so clearly exhibited a commitment to improve the parity of the children's participation in quality education. He believed that his openness to the views of the children in his school actively enhanced the effectiveness of his teaching.

Another teacher, who had attended the original workshops and with whom we later reconnected, openly described the teachers' general lack of awareness of the specific challenges facing the children in their care. Reflecting on the earlier workshops, she observed: 'We were completely unaware of these issues' (interview, April 2022). Although the teachers are themselves refugees, they are less likely to be still living in the informal tented settlements in Lebanon where many of their children were still housed. Indeed, as educated working professionals employed by an NGO, they are likely to have different daily living experiences from those of the refugee children.

This teacher noted that she and her colleagues listened receptively to the ideas suggested by the children for improving their learning experiences. In some cases, this meant acknowledging how they might have inadvertently displayed negative attitudes toward their pupils and adapting their classroom behaviours accordingly. In an interview in April 2022, she commented:

> We worked on improving ourselves and our practices. For example, some students said that this teacher is always angry, this teacher is shy, etc. Hence, we worked on improving ourselves and tried to mitigate these negative practices.

This teacher went on to explain how children who typically struggled with their learning had been further marginalised by the absence of good relations with the teachers. She described the positive impact of re-establishing a connection based on care and attention:

> In every classroom, you will find students at different levels [of attainment]; however, once you achieve a good relationship, low levels of learning become less [widespread] … Some of my students love me but they do not do well in class. Nevertheless, once they feel my love and care, they become more involved and work harder because love will keep them in class and so they will succeed eventually.

This teacher has clearly moved toward a framework of care in building human relationships with the children by conceptualising the process of truly listening and recognising the children's lived experiences. This resonates with the model of 'pedagogical love' posited by Kaukko et al. (2021), as noted in Chapter 5. This same teacher worked to build relationships even during the restrictions of previous years, on occasion even visiting her pupils during and after the lockdown periods to ascertain how she might better support them in their specific circumstances. In spite of the online learning modality, she continued to maintain contact with parents and caregivers, as well as children, through mobile phone messaging, creating an opportunity to keep channels of communication open outside the confines of the short school 'shift' times.

For her, finding opportunities to engage with the learners was not always easy but was largely worthwhile in terms of children remaining in school, achieving better educational outcomes and feeling seen and understood as individuals. This is a powerful example of the positive impact teachers can potentially have when open to children expressing their needs, rather than their needs being inferred by adults – in line with Noddings' (2005) framing (see Chapter 2). The role of love and care is not only central to a sense of safety and belonging within education, as highlighted here, but also an aspect of social justice that resonates with the insights of the Syrian children now living and attending schools in London who were presented in Chapter 5 of this book.

It is, of course, too soon to know the longer-term impacts of children being denied access not only to learning opportunities but also, perhaps more importantly, to the safety of the school routine and the sense of belonging and success that school can ideally provide, which children say they value so much (Kohli, 2006; 2011; 2014). Whatever the future effects may be, Syrian children such as those we met in Lebanon and London have already experienced multiple and complex injustices, as described throughout this book. The phrase 'now more than ever' has arguably been overused in relation to the COVID-19 pandemic and 'post-COVID' reflections. However, to begin creating the groundwork for improved social justice through education for children caught in the nexus of overlapping catastrophes, we must start allowing them to represent their devastating and resilient life experiences. Some teachers of these very children have shown us how this might be possible, even without structured support or resources. Their work and the results of our research underpinning this book could – or maybe should – be relevant for all those genuinely seeking to nurture and support some of the most vulnerable among our global society. To clarify, social justice means we must let the children represent their own experiences. We must listen, they must be heard, and their expressed needs must be acted upon (Lundy, 2007).

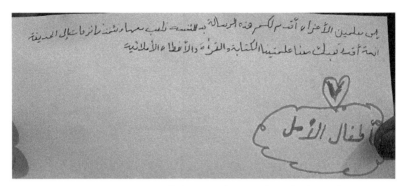

Figure 8.1   A MAPs pupil's letter to their teacher. © The authors.

To the dear teachers

I dedicate this letter to you, I want the teacher to play with us and take us for picnics to the park. Miss, I appreciate your efforts with us, you taught us to write and read and [showed us] our spelling mistakes.

Child of Hope

8
Transforming education to empower displaced children

Throughout this book, we have presented the testimonies of children in different contexts. Thanks to their perspectives and insights, they have revealed much about their current (at the time of research) situations and have had many things to tell us about what they think of the nature and quality of their education provision, as well as their sense of belonging and community. In this final part of the book, we would like to reflect a little further on what these children have shared with us and taught us, and to consider the broader implications of those lessons for teachers, schools, education-system designers, donors and policymakers.

We will conclude by arguing that developing such activities in mainstream formal and NFE programmes alike is likely to require transformations in views on learning and in pedagogical relationships between teachers and children. The following section illustrates the contextual factors of mainstream education for Syrian refugee children in Lebanon in particular (but relevant also to those within the English education landscape) that inherently deprive them of, and even prevent the design of, empowering pedagogies.

Education contexts that marginalise and disempower children

Schools and other formal and NFE contexts in Lebanon and the UK are, for the most part, characterised by a dominant essentialist pedagogical culture. As a philosophy of education, essentialism emphasises the acquisition of knowledge that higher authorities deem essential and ensure acquisition through standardised testing (Hirsch, 1988).

The selected knowledge is then presented to children as absolute or final. In other words, children have virtually no opportunity to learn how this knowledge was constructed or how to use this knowledge to build new meanings, arguments or solutions. Hence, the learning modalities primarily demand that children accurately recall information and learn procedural knowledge through repetition. Freire (1970) illustrated this pedagogical experience as 'banking' information with children as receptacles, meaning that they are denied the opportunity to question sources, to deliberate, and to access other such components of critical pedagogies. Learning spaces that exhibit such pedagogical cultures are also typically observed in conflict-affected LMICs such as Iraq (Mohammed-Marzouk, 2012), Liberia (Quaynor, 2015), Egypt (Hargreaves & Elhawary, 2021), Rwanda, Kosovo, Croatia and Bosnia and Herzegovina (Weinstein et al., 2007).

A results-based, knowledge-transmission education culture – in which test scores end up as the primary measures of success or achievement – is unjust. Accountability mechanisms that place schools and teachers in the spotlight have shaped feedback that emphasises attainment in tests rather than effort, creativity or criticality. Moreover, children who require more time or additional resources because of particular needs or disabilities are often either segregated or even removed from school altogether. Children who have access to healthy food and regular meals and sleep, who live in safe and emotionally nourishing homes and communities and whose caregivers can afford tutor support have a massive advantage when it comes to attaining/ retaining knowledge and, thus, performing well in tests. In other words, the dominant pedagogical culture of transmitting knowledge prevents the fundamental opportunities for parity-of-participation.

Pedagogies that embrace the knowledge and capital that any child brings to the classroom and recognise the emotional and social learning and struggles of each child therefore constitute *expressions* of redistribution, recognition and representation. Only through this kind of environment can children experience the safety and feel the sense of belonging that help foster long-term achievement, as per Kohli's (2011) schema (see Figure 8.2). Furthermore, the absence of these expressions is indicative of an authoritarian-like education system that sustains exclusion and social injustice.

Figure 8.2 'Myself in ten years' by a Syrian refugee pupil at a MAPs education centre. © The authors.

Transforming pedagogies

The children's struggles in compounded crises, such as those we have discussed in the case of Lebanon, coupled with pedagogies that demand that children quickly recall information, undermine education's role in ensuring that children have more fair and equitable opportunities to participate, whether during or beyond their schooling. Within these two factors – compounded crises and disempowering pedagogies – we, educationists, can influence the learning and social and emotional experiences of children. Such a pedagogy for social justice would necessitate a transformation in how we approach learning and children, in a shift away from the pedagogical cultures of knowledge transmission and low expectations of children that merely ask them to recite or recall. The following sections of this final chapter outline two broad areas for attention that can facilitate such a transformation: away from a pedagogical culture that marginalises children from parity-of-participation and towards one that empowers them through their increased representation, recognition of their value, and redistribution of learning opportunities. All of these steps can contribute to their organic sense of safety, belonging and achievement.

Reconstructing time, hierarchy and knowledge

Such transformations inevitably start with smaller changes, which can begin to happen when leaders, teachers and caregivers reconstruct time, hierarchy and knowledge. Allocating time means more systemically opening up spaces for meaningful teacher–learner dialogue, while reconstructing time includes re-questioning how much time we give children to try to solve problems, find evidence, carry out work with a peer, read a text or write. To reshape hierarchy in the classroom is to flatten the power dynamics so that teachers and children truly become partners in the learning journey (as noted by children in Chapters 4 and 5). As partners, children bring (and often are) resources for the class to examine and set challenges for all pupils to solve. Teachers' questions to children can be open-ended and genuinely provoke deeper understanding rather than simply test how much knowledge was retained.

Knowledge itself can be reconstructed and co-constructed, extending beyond the limited diet of literacy and numeracy that, all too often, is the extent of provision for those already educationally deprived. Knowledge that derives from the powerful – knowledge that governing authorities dictate as essential – may further marginalise under-represented children who can potentially bring and build on their own 'powerful knowledge' that aligns their understandings with their surrounding realities (Young, 2008). Of course, for parity-of-participation and empowerment, children usually need strong commands of literacy and numeracy. However, pedagogical activities can disempower and marginalise when children are positioned as uncritical receivers of that knowledge or information. So knowledge can and should be reconstructed for breadth and relevance, bringing children into their birthright of human culture, experience and learning; but, for social justice to be embraced, it should also be reconstructed so that it empowers learners as critical thinkers, creative innovators and problem-solvers. Further, as was so clearly demonstrated in the MAPs research workshops that formed the core of this book (see Chapter 4), knowledge of learning and growth itself can be developed and communicated, with children documenting and reflecting on how they have learned and developed as self-critical, creative inquirers, and effectively communicating to peers and teachers so that their support is more aligned with intentions to learn better.

Teacher agency through inspiration, knowledge and risk

The challenges faced by teachers, in general, and teachers who work with refugee children in particular, are immense. However, during the compounded crises, including the issues surrounding the COVID-19 pandemic and school closures in particular, teachers in many educational settings have demonstrated their capacity to exercise agency. For example, they took the initiative to create classrooms via WhatsApp, source appropriate learning materials and make necessary practical arrangements with parents.

However, the agency that is critical for transforming a pedagogical culture will also require teachers to build or even reconstruct knowledge of child development and learning. Fewer than a quarter of teachers in Lebanon, in particular, have teaching qualifications (CERD, 2020). In the case of the UK, many educators who are responsible for teaching refugee children lack sustainable and consistent approaches to training and professional development and rely instead on ad-hoc and fragile responses that deprive refugee children of adequate forms of education that cater to their needs (Prentice & Ott, 2021). Hence, we can safely assume that, among the teacher workforce, there is limited evidence-informed knowledge of how neglect and violence influence children's cognitive, socio-emotional, linguistic and physical development (see Chapters 3 and 5). Furthermore, the approaches that emphasise the requirement for children to retain information through repetition are sustained by teachers' classroom practices, in addition to systems of accountability and performance that require teachers to favour quantity over quality in education. Therefore, teacher agency needs a redirection. Testimonials and other stories of transformation in the learning of displaced children can inspire teachers to critically examine their own practices and possibly experiment with other approaches.

However, our call – shared by like-minded educators – is not just for new ideas, for different methodologies or for more meaningful training. Crucially, it is for teachers to be adequately trained and granted the agency to actually implement changes in classroom practice that arise from such professional development. There is no point in such training or enhanced awareness of the importance of the child's context and needs if teachers are not allowed the freedom (and support) in their schools and classrooms to actually enact change. In other words, there is no return on the investment of time and resources in building capacity among teachers, a seemingly permanent feature in humanitarian donors' agendas, if they are then denied the opportunity to deploy that enhanced capacity.

Further, a model of awareness-raising and capacity-building married with denial of practical implementation does not accord with the principles of 'doing no harm'. This is an ethical aspect that must be particularly considered in contexts where the teachers are, themselves, facing vulnerable, agency-denying circumstances – such as those of the Syrian refugee teachers of Syrian refugee children in Lebanon. Therefore, our call must also extend to training and development in these areas for education-system leaders, school principals and supervisors, along the same lines as for classroom teachers. It should be obvious that school leaders at all levels are vital to the openness to transforma-tion of education provision, yet they are so often left out of professional development opportunities or have change imposed upon them without serious attempts to include them in understanding and shaping the process. Moreover, school leaders' limited degrees of autonomy and resources significantly restrict school-based practitioners' intentions to include refugee children in mainstream activities and help address the traumas of poverty and war-related forced displacement, as in the case of Turkey (Arar & Örücü, 2022). If teachers are to be able to try out new ideas to allow social justice to flourish through playing their part in securing parity-of-participation and supporting belonging and safety in their classrooms, then education leaders must know, accept and facilitate this proposed direction of travel among the teachers for whom they are responsible.

Experimenting with different pedagogies poses a risk for teachers and caregivers, who may not feel confident about the idea of children constructing knowledge by themselves or with their peers. Parents, similarly, may not know how to create the right spaces in which children can solve problems at home or how to give feedback that educates rather than provides final answers. To channel the agency of parents and teachers toward a pathway that engages children as knowledge-makers, educationists will need to consider providing periodic coaching for school leaders, teachers and caregivers, in addition to the training mentioned earlier. This would be a more reactive and tailored set of interventions. A caregiver and teacher coaching curriculum could include evidence-informed understandings of child development (including evidence from children themselves), the impacts of harm on development and learning, and approaches to effective learning.

In many cases, and in contexts all around the world (not just in 'education in emergency' settings), this will require a cultural shift in attitudes to learning and education at community level, and the authors of this book do not underestimate the magnitude of that task. It is very common for families to have deeply ingrained views of what 'proper' schooling should look like, often based on their own experiences as young learners and with a deep veneration for that tradition. This model of expected reproduction – often defaulting to strong didactic, authoritarian dynamics within teaching spaces and with a clear essentialist pedagogical culture (as outlined, for example, in Chapter 6) – will only be dismantled through careful and sensitive work with families and their broader communities. We acknowledge that such moves present a potential risk to the trust required between school and home. Additionally, there is risk attached to the teachers themselves trying out new ideas in the classroom, especially when done against a prevailing culture of not questioning authority (related to the issues noted by the teachers who shared their reflections in Chapter 7). Teachers would be required to make themselves 'vulnerable' to their pupils through being open to their feedback; and they might also feel a similar vulnerability in relation to their colleagues, as well as their bosses, parents and the wider communities in which they work. But such vulnerabilities are exactly the means through which powerful professional learning and transformation might take place, to the great benefit of the children's development and capacity to enjoy social justice in and through their learning.

It must also be acknowledged that there is a further risk to the schools themselves. On an institutional level, formal schools in many national contexts (including Lebanon and the UK) are bound to and judged within a system of public assessment that unnecessarily rewards the toxic pedagogies of recall and repetition – even though high attainment can be achieved through humane and child-centred ways. So consideration must be given to how to persuade school principals to allow classroom changes that they perceive as potential risks to their schools' reputations (both locally and with national education authorities). This brings us back to our call for working with education-system leaders to ensure that, as far as they are able, schools are leveraging rather than stymying children's creative, critical learning and, thereby, their access to social justice.

Educating refugees: what children have to tell us and why it matters

The transformation we authors propose toward a socially-just education landscape through parity-of-participation requires us to uplift children and see them as holders and creative co-constructors of knowledge, critical thinkers and agency-wielding problem-solvers. They can be all these things and more when they are helped to develop strong senses of belonging, safety and recognised success. Such a move has the potential to transform the experiences in and through education for all children, and especially the most vulnerable and marginalised among them, such as those it has been our privilege to meet and learn from in the preparation of this book (see Figures 8.3 and 8.4).

Figure 8.3 'School of Hope' by a Syrian refugee pupil at a MAPs education centre. © The authors.

Figure 8.4 A MAPs pupil's letter to their teacher. © The authors.

My dearest teachers

For the sake of future students, I suggest that:
I love my teacher because she is great and loves everyone and I appreciate her for
that, and I love all the teachers who are like her. I appreciate your efforts and your
hard work [my teacher]. Thank you!
I love you.

From Children of Hope

References

Abu Moghli, M. & Shuayb, M. (2020). *Education under COVID-19 lockdown: Reflections from teachers, students and parents*. Centre for Lebanese Studies, Lebanese American University. https://leba nesestudies.com/wp-content/uploads/2020/06/booklet-covid-19eng-4augFinal.pdf

Akar, B. (2019). *Citizenship education in conflict-affected areas: Lebanon and beyond*. Bloomsbury Academic.

Akar, B. (2021). *Basic education in Lebanon: Rapid education and risk analysis and social inclusion analysis (RERA + SI)*. World Learning Lebanon. https://pdf.usaid.gov/pdf_docs/PA00ZTN1. pdf

Akar, B. & Albrecht, M. (2017). Influences of nationalisms on citizenship education: Revealing a 'dark side' in Lebanon. *Nations and Nationalism, 23*(3), 547–570. https://doi.org/10.1111/ nana.12316

Akar, B., & Van Ommering, E. (2018). An emerging framework for providing education to Syrian refugee children in Lebanon. In M. Pace & S. Sen (Eds.), *Syrian refugee children in the Middle East and Europe: Integrating the young and exiled* (pp. 59–72). Routledge.

Anderson, A., Hamilton, R., Moore, D., Loewen, S. & Frater-Mathieson, K. (2004). Education of refugee children: Theoretical perspectives and best practice. In R. Hamilton & D. Moore (Eds.), *Educational interventions for refugee children: Theoretical perspectives and implementing best practice* (pp. 1–11). Taylor & Francis.

Arar, K. & Örücü, D. (2022). Post-migration ecology in educational leadership and policy for social justice: Welcoming refugee students in two distinct national contexts. *Educational Management Administration & Leadership, 0*(0), 1–24. https://doi.org/10.1177/174114322 21136404

Arnot, M. & Pinson, H. (2005). *The education of asylum-seeker and refugee children: A study of LEA and school values, policies and practices*. Faculty of Education, University of Cambridge. https://www.educ.cam.ac.uk/people/staff/arnot/AsylumReportFinal.pdf

Arnstein, S. R. (1969). A ladder of citizen participation. *Journal of the American Institute of Planners, 35*(4), 216–224.

Aziz, C., Harb, N., Ahmadieh, S. E., Kazan, W. & Feghaly, Y. E. (2020). An integrated social and emotional learning framework for Lebanese schools. In C. Cefai, D. Regester & L. Akoury-Dirani (Eds.), *Social and emotional learning in the Mediterranean: Cross cultural perspectives and approaches* (pp. 83–98). Brill.

Baumeister, R. F. & Leary, M. R. (1995). The need to belong: Desire for interpersonal attachments as a fundamental human motivation. *Psychological Bulletin, 117*(3), 497–529. https://doi. org/10.1037/0033-2909.117.3.497

BBC. (2020, 5 August). Lebanon: Why the country is in crisis. https://www.bbc.com/news/ world-middle-east-53390108

Berry, J. W. (1997). Immigration, acculturation, and adaptation. *Applied Psychology, 46*(1), 5–34. https://doi.org/https://doi.org/10.1111/j.1464-0597.1997.tb01087.x

Berry, J. W. (2005). Acculturation: Living successfully in two cultures. *International Journal of Intercultural Relations, 29*(6), 697–712. https://doi.org/https://doi.org/10.1016/j. ijintrel.2005.07.013

Berry, J. W. (2009). A critique of critical acculturation. *International Journal of Intercultural Relations, 33*(5), 361–371. https://doi.org/https://doi.org/10.1016/j.ijintrel.2009.06.003

Betancourt, T. S., Simmons, S., Borisova, I., Brewer, S. E., Iweala, U. & de la Soudière, M. (2008). High hopes, grim reality: Reintegration and the education of former child soldiers in Sierra Leone. *Comparative Education Review, 52*(4), 565–587. https://doi.org/10.1086/ 591298

Brock, C. (2011). *Education as a global concern*. Continuum.

Buckner, E. & Spencer, D. (2016). *Educating Syrian refugees in Lebanon*. Carnegie Endowment for Peace. http://carnegieendowment.org/sada/?fa=63513.

Bush, K. D. & Saltarelli, D. (2000). *The two faces of education in ethnic conflict: Towards a peace-building education for children*. UNICEF, Innocenti Research Centre. https://www.unicef-irc.org/publications/pdf/insight4.pdf

Center on the Developing Child. (2011). *Building the brain's 'air traffic control' system: How early experiences shape the development of executive function* (Working Paper No. 11). http://www.developingchild.harvard.edu

CERD. (2014). *Statistical bulletin: Academic year 2013–2014*. https://t.ly/fsQv2 [Arabic]

CERD. (2019). *Statistical bulletin: Academic year 2018–2019*. http://crdp.org/files/201908 300826465.pdf [Arabic]

CERD. (2020). *Statistical bulletin: Academic year 2019–2020*. https://www.crdp.org/sites/default/files/2020-09/202008281054095_0.pdf [Arabic]

Chinnery, J. & Akar, B. (2021). *Resilience in the return to learning during COVID-19: Lebanon case study*. United States Agency for International Development. https://www.eccnetwork.net/sites/default/files/media/file/Resilience%20In%20Return%20to%20Learning%20During%20Covid-19%20Lebanon%20Case%20Study.pdf

Cohen, J. (2001). Social and emotional education: Core principles and practices. In J. Cohen (Ed.), *Caring classrooms/intelligent schools: The social emotional education of young children* (pp. 3–29). Teachers College Press.

Culbertson, S. & Constant, L. (2015). *Education of Syrian Refugee Children: Managing the crisis in Turkey, Lebanon, and Jordan*. RAND Corporation.

Deane, S. (2016). Syria's lost generation: Refugee education provision and societal security in an ongoing conflict emergency. *IDS Bulletin, 47*(3), 35–52. http://bulletin.ids.ac.uk/idsbo/article/view/2729/HTML

DfES. (2003). *Every child matters*. HMSO. https://assets.publishing.service.gov.uk/media/5a7c95 a4e5274a0bb7cb806d/5860.pdf

Dryden-Peterson, S., Adelman, E., Bellino, M. J. & Chopra, V. (2019). The purposes of refugee education: Policy and practice of including refugees in national education systems. *Sociology of Education, 92*(4), 346–366. https://doi.org/10.1177/0038040719863054

Due, C., Riggs, D. W. & Augoustinos, M. (2016). Experiences of school belonging for young children with refugee backgrounds. *The Educational and Developmental Psychologist, 33*(1), 33–53. https://doi.org/10.1017/edp.2016.9

EEF (2023) *The EEF Guide to the pupil premium: How to plan, implement, monitor, and sustain an effective strategy*. Education Endowment Foundation. https://d2tic4wvo1iusb.cloudfront.net/production/documents/guidance-for-teachers/pupil-premium/Pupil-Premium-2023.pdf?v=1696434151.

El-Amine, A. (2004). Educational reform: Nine principles and five issues. In N. Salam (Ed.), *Options for Lebanon* (pp. 209–254). Centre for Lebanese Studies and I.B. Tauris.

El-Zein, A., DeJong, J., Fargues, P., Salti, N., Hanieh, A. & Lackner, H. (2016). Who's been left behind? Why sustainable development goals fail the Arab world. *The Lancet, 388*(10040), 207–210. https://doi.org/10.1016/S0140-6736(15)01312-4

Errighi, L. & Griesse, J. (2016). *The Syrian refugee crisis: Labour market implications in Jordan and Lebanon* (European Economy Discussion Paper, 29). https://economy-finance.ec.europa.eu/system/files/2020-06/dp029_en.pdf

European Parliament. (2022). *Situation in Lebanon: Severe and prolonged economic depression* (Think Tank Briefing, Issue 13 April). https://www.europarl.europa.eu/thinktank/en/document/EPRS_BRI(2022)729369

Fraser, N. (2001). Recognition without ethics? *Theory, Culture & Society, 18*(2), 21–42. https://doi.org/10.1177/02632760122051760

Fraser, N. (2008). *Scales of justice: Reimagining political space in a globalizing world*. Polity Press.

Fraser, N. (2018). Recognition without ethics? In C. McKinnon & D. Castiglione (Eds.), *The Culture of Toleration in Diverse Societies* (pp. 21–42). Manchester University Press.

Fraser, N. (2019). *The old is dying and the new cannot be born: From progressive neoliberalism to Trump and beyond*. Verso.

Frayha, N. (2010). Pressure groups, education policy, and curriculum development in Lebanon: A policy maker's retrospective and introspective standpoint. In A. E. Mazawi & R. G. Sultana (Eds.), *Education and the Arab 'World': Political projects, struggles, and geometries of power* (pp. 93–113). Routledge.

Freire, P. (2017 [1970]). *Pedagogy of the oppressed*, trans. M. Bergman Ramos (13th ed.). Penguin Random House.

Harber, C. (2004). *Schooling as violence: How schools harm pupils and societies*. RoutledgeFalmer.

Hargreaves, E. & Elhawary, D. (2021). Children's experiences of agency when learning English in the classroom of a collectivist culture. *System*, *98*, 102476. https://doi.org/10.1016/j. system.2021.102476.

Hargreaves, E., Elhawary, D. & Mahgoub, M. (2018). Children critique learning the 'pure' subject of English in the traditional classroom. *Educational Studies*, *44*(5), 535–550. https://doi.org/ 10.1080/03055698.2017.1382329

Hart, B. & Risley, T. R. (1992). American parenting of language-learning children: Persisting differences in family-child interactions observed in natural home environments. *Developmental Psychology*, *28*(6), 1096–1105. https://doi.org/10.1037/0012-1649.28.6.1096

Hart, B. & Risley, T. R. (1995). *Meaningful differences in the everyday experience of young American children*. Paul H. Brookes.

Hart, J. (2004). *Children's participation in humanitarian action: Learning from zones of armed conflict*. Refugee Studies Centre, University of Oxford. https://inee.org/sites/default/files/ Childrens_Participation_in_Humanitarian_Act_EN.PDF

Hirsch, E. D. (1988). *Cultural literacy: What every American needs to know*. Random House.

hooks, b. (1994). *Teaching to transgress: Education as the practice of freedom*. Routledge.

hooks, b. (2000). *All about love: New visions*. William Morrow and Company.

Human Rights Watch. (2016). *Growing up without an education: Barriers to education for Syrian refugee children in Lebanon*. https://www.hrw.org/sites/default/files/report_pdf/lebanon 0716web_1.pdf

Human Rights Watch. (2019). *'I don't want my child to be beaten': Corporal punishment in Lebanon's schools*. https://www.hrw.org/sites/default/files/report_pdf/lebanon0519_web2.pdf

Human Rights Watch. (2022). *Lebanon: Credible plans needed on education crisis*. https://www. hrw.org/news/2022/05/06/lebanon-credible-plans-needed-education-crisis

Immerstein, S. & Al-Shaikhly, S. (2016). *Education in Syria*. World Education Services. http:// wenr.wes.org/2016/04/education-in-syria

INEE. (2010). *Minimum standards for education: Preparedness, response, recovery* (2nd ed.). International Network for Education in Emergencies. https://inee.org/sites/default/files/ resources/INEE_Minimum_Standards_Handbook_2010%28HSP%29_EN.pdf

INEE. (2014). *Lebanon—Minimum standards for education in emergencies: Contextualized from the INEE Minimum Standards for Education: Preparedness, response, recovery*. INEE and Lebanon Education Working Group. https://inee.org/sites/default/files/resources/INEE_MS_Context ualized_Lebanon_English_2014.pdf

INEE. (2022). *EiE Glossary*. https://inee.org/eie-glossary/primary-education

International Rescue Committee. (2016). *Overview of right to work for refugees—Syria Crisis Response: Lebanon and Jordan*. https://www.rescue.org/sites/default/files/document/987/ policybrief2righttoworkforrefugees-syriacrisisresponsejanuary25.pdf

Janmyr, M. (2017). No country of asylum: 'Legitimizing' Lebanon's rejection of the 1951 Refugee Convention. *International Journal of Refugee Law*, *29*(3), 438–465. https://doi.org/10.1093/ ijrl/eex026

Jones, K. & Ksaifi, L. (2016). *Struggling to survive: Slavery and exploitation of Syrian refugees in Lebanon*. Freedom Fund. https://freedomfund.org/wp-content/uploads/Lebanon-Report-FINAL-8April16.pdf

Jung, H. & Hasan, A. (2016). The impact of early childhood education on early achievement gaps in Indonesia. *Journal of Development Effectiveness*, *8*(2), 216–233. https://doi.org/10.1080/1 9439342.2015.1088054

Karam, F. J., Monaghan, C. & Yoder, P. J. (2016). 'The students do not know why they are here': Education decision-making for Syrian refugees. *Globalisation, Societies and Education*, *15*(4), 448–463. https://doi.org/10.1080/14767724.2016.1222895

Kaukko, M., Wilkinson, J. & Kohli, R. K. (2021). Pedagogical love in Finland and Australia: A study of refugee children and their teachers. *Pedagogy, Culture & Society*, *30*(3), 1–17. https://doi. org/10.1080/14681366.2020.1868555

Keddie, A. (2012). Schooling and social justice through the lenses of Nancy Fraser. *Critical Studies in Education*, *53*(3), 263–279. https://doi.org/10.1080/17508487.2012. 709185

Kelly, N. (2017). Responding to a refugee influx: Lessons from Lebanon. *Journal on Migration and Human Security*, *5*(1), 82–104.

Kingdon G. G., Little, A., Aslam, M., Rawal, S., Moe, T., Patrinos, H., Beteille, T., Banerji, R., Parton, B. & Sharma, S. K. (2014). *A rigorous review of the political economy of education systems in developing countries*. Education Rigorous Literature Review. UK Department for International Development. https://eppi.ioe.ac.uk/cms/Portals/0/PDF%20reviews%20and%20summaries/Political%20economy%202014Kingdon.pdf?ver=2014-04-24-141259-443

Kohli, R. K. S. (2006). The sound of silence: Listening to what unaccompanied asylum-seeking children say and do not say. *British Journal of Social Work*, *36*(5), 707–721. https://doi.org/10.1093/bjsw/bch305

Kohli, R. K. S. (2011). Working to ensure safety, belonging and success for unaccompanied asylum-seeking children. *Child Abuse Review*, *20*(5), 311–323. https://doi.org/https://doi.org/10.1002/car.1182

Kohli, R. K. S. (2014). Protecting asylum seeking children on the move. *Revue européenne des migrations internationales*, *30*(1), 83–104.

Kutsyuruba, B., Klinger, D. A. & Hussain, A. (2015). Relationships among school climate, school safety, and student achievement and well-being: A review of the literature. *Review of Education*, *3*(2), 103–135. https://doi.org/https://doi.org/10.1002/rev3.3043

Lenette, C. (2019). *Arts-based methods in refugee research: Creating sanctuary*. Springer.

Loft, P., Sturge, G. and Kirk-Wade, E. (2023). The Syrian Civil War: Timeline and statistics. *House of Commons Library*. https://researchbriefings.files.parliament.uk/documents/CBP-9381/CBP-9381.pdf.

Lundy, L. (2007). 'Voice' is not enough: Conceptualising Article 12 of the United Nations Convention on the Rights of the Child. *British Educational Research Journal*, *33*(6), 927–942. https://doi.org/https://doi.org/10.1080/01411920701657033

Lundy, L. (2012). Children's rights and educational policy in Europe: The implementation of the United Nations Convention on the Rights of the Child. *Oxford Review of Education*, *38*(4), 393–411. https://doi.org/10.1080/03054985.2012.704874

Maxwell, J. A. (2012). *Qualitative research design: An interactive approach*. Sage.

May, V. (2015). When recognition fails: Mass observation project accounts of not belonging. *Sociology*, *50*(4), 748–763. https://doi.org/10.1177/0038038515578991

McIntyre, J. & Abrams, F. (2021). *Refugee education: Theorising practice in schools*. Routledge.

McIntyre, J. & Hall, C. (2018). Barriers to the inclusion of refugee and asylum-seeking children in schools in England. *Educational Review*, *72*(5), 583–600. https://doi.org/10.1080/00131911.2018.1544115

McIntyre, J. & Neuhaus, S. (2021). Theorising policy and practice in refugee education: Conceptualising 'safety', 'belonging', 'success' and 'participatory parity' in England and Sweden. *British Educational Research Journal*, *47*(4), 796–816. https://doi.org/https://doi.org/10.1002/berj.3701

McIntyre, J., Neuhaus, S., and Blennow, K. (2020). Participatory parity in schooling and moves towards ordinariness: A comparison of refugee education policy and practice in England and Sweden. *Compare: A Journal of Comparative and International Education*, *50*(3), 391–409. https://doi.org/10.1080/03057925.2018.1515007.

MEHE. (1997). *The programs of general education and their aims*.

MEHE. (2010). *Quality education for growth: National education strategy framework: Education sector development plan (general education): 2010–2015*. http://planipolis.iiep.unesco.org/upload/Lebanon/Lebanon_ESDP_2010-2015.pdf

MEHE (2014) *Reaching all children with education in Lebanon*. https://www.mehe.gov.lb/ar/Projects/العام%20التعليم/RACEfinalEnglish2.pdf.

MEHE. (2016). *Reaching all children with education: RACE II (2017–2021)*. https://planipolis.iiep.unesco.org/sites/default/files/ressources/lebanon_race-ii_2017-2021.pdf

Menashy, F. & Zakharia, Z. (2022). Crisis upon crisis: Refugee education responses amid COVID-19. *Peabody Journal of Education*, *97*(3), 309–325. https://doi.org/10.1080/0161956X.2022.2079895

Mohammed-Marzouk, M. R. (2012). Teaching and learning in Iraq: A brief history. *The Educational Forum*, *76*(2), 259–264. https://doi.org/10.1080/00131725.2011.653869

Multi-Aid Programs. (2019). *Children of Hope* (video). https://youtu.be/Z7ZUOw0O_wk.

Nahmias, P. & Baal, N. K. (2019). *Including forced displacement in the SDGs: A new refugee indicator*. UNHCR blog post. https://www.unhcr.org/blogs/including-forced-displacement-in-the-sdgs-a-new-refugee-indicator/

National Scientific Council on the Developing Child. (2004). *Young children develop in an environment of relationships* (Working Paper No. 1). https://developingchild.harvard.edu/wp-content/uploads/2004/04/Young-Children-Develop-in-an-Environment-of-Relationships.pdf

National Scientific Council on the Developing Child. (2007). *The timing and quality of early experiences combine to shape brain architecture* (Working Paper No. 5). https://harvardcenter.wpenginepowered.com/wp-content/uploads/2007/05/Timing_Quality_Early_Experiences-1.pdf

Nelson, C. A., Fox, N. A. & Zeanah, C. H. (2013). Anguish of the abandoned child. *Scientific American, 308*(4), 62–67.

Noddings, N. (2005). Identifying and responding to needs in education. *Cambridge Journal of Education, 35*(2), 147–159. https://doi.org/10.1080/03057640500146757

Novelli, M., Lopes Cardozo, M. & Smith, A. (2015). A theoretical framework for analysing the contribution of education to sustainable peacebuilding: 4Rs in conflict-affected contexts. *Research Consortium on Education and Peacebuilding.* https://pure.uva.nl/ws/files/44045793/2591292.pdf

Novelli, M., Lopes Cardozo, M. & Smith, A. (2019). The '4 Rs' as a tool for critical policy analysis of the education sector in conflict affected states. *Education and Conflict Review, 2*, 70–75. https://discovery.ucl.ac.uk/id/eprint/10081589/1/Novelli_Article_12_Novelli.pdf

Olson, K. (2008). Participatory parity and democratic justice. In K. Olson (Ed.), *Adding insult to injury: Nancy Fraser debates her critics* (pp. 246–272). Verso.

Örücü, D., Arar, K. & Mahfouz, J. (2021). Three contexts as the post-migration ecology for refugees: School principals' challenges and strategies in Turkey, Lebanon, and Germany. *Leadership and Policy in Schools, 20*(1), 41–56. https://doi:10.1080/15700763.2020.1833044.

Osler, A. (2016). *Human rights and schooling: An ethical framework for teaching for social justice.* Teachers College Press.

Pinson, H. & Arnot, M. (2007). Sociology of education and the wasteland of refugee education research. *British Journal of Sociology of Education, 28*(3), 399–407. https://doi.org/10.1080/01425690701253612

Pinson, H., Arnot, M. & Candappa, M. (2010). *Education, asylum and the 'non-citizen' child: The politics of compassion and belonging.* Palgrave Macmillan.

Power, S. (2012). From redistribution to recognition to representation: Social injustice and the changing politics of education. *Globalisation, Societies and Education, 10*(4), 473–492. https://doi.org/10.1080/14767724.2012.735154

Prentice, C. M. & Ott, E. (2021). Previous experience, trickle-down training and systemic ad hoc-ery: Educators' knowledge acquisition when teaching refugee pupils in one local authority in England. *Teachers and Teaching: Theory and Practice, 27*(1), 269–283. https://doi.org/10.1080/13540602.2021.1946034

Quaynor, L. (2015). 'I do not have the means to speak': Educating youth for citizenship in post-conflict Liberia. *Journal of Peace Education, 12*(1), 15–36. https://doi.org/10.1080/17400201.2014.931277

Roorda, D. L., Koomen, H. M. Y., Spilt, J. L. & Oort, F. J. (2011). The influence of affective teacher–student relationships on students' school engagement and achievement: A meta-analytic approach. *Review of Educational Research, 81*(4), 493–529. https://doi.org/10.3102/0034654311421793

Rudduck, J. & Flutter, J. (2004). *How to improve your school.* Continuum.

Save the Children. (2021). *Lebanon's child survival crisis: Time to act.* https://resourcecentre.savethechildren.net/pdf/lebanons_child_survival_crisis_external_briefing_final.docx.pdf/

Schwartz, S. J., Unger, J. B., Zamboanga, B. L. & Szapocznik, J. (2010). Rethinking the concept of acculturation: Implications for theory and research. *American Psychologist, 65*(4), 237–251. https://doi.org/10.1037/a0019330

Sen, A. (1992). *Inequality reexamined.* Oxford University Press.

Shonkoff, J. P., Garner, A. S., Siegel, B. S., Dobbins, M. I., Earls, M. F., Garner, A. S., McGuinn, L., Pascoe, J., Wood, D. L., High, P. C., Donoghue, E., Fussell, J. J., Gleason, M. M., Jaudes,

P. K., Jones, V. F., Rubin, D. M., Schulte, E. E., Macias, M. M., Bridgemohan, C., Fussell, J., Goldson, E., McGuinn, L. J., Weitzman, C. & Wegner, L. M. (2012). The lifelong effects of early childhood adversity and toxic stress. *Pediatrics, 129*(1), e232–246. https://doi.org/10.1542/peds.2011-2663

Shuayb, M., Hammoud, M., Al-Samhoury, O. & Durgham, N. (2020). *Invisible barriers: Factors influencing Syrian refugee youth in continuing their education in Lebanon.* Jusoor and Centre for Lebanese Studies. https://lebanesestudies.com/wp-content/uploads/2021/03/Jusoor-Brevet-2020-Report.pdf

Shuayb, M., Makkouk, N. & Tuttunji, S. (2014). *Widening access to quality education for Syrian refugees: The role of private and NGO sectors in Lebanon.* Centre for Lebanese Studies. https://lebanesestudies.com/wp-content/uploads/2014/09/Widening-Access-to-Quality-Education-for-Syrian-Refugees-the-role-private-and-NGO-sectors-in-Lebanon-.pdf

Sidhu, R. & Taylor, S. (2007). Educational provision for refugee youth in Australia: Left to chance? *Sociology of Education, 43*(3), 283–300. https://doi.org/10.1177/1440783307080107

Starkey, H. (2012). Human rights, cosmopolitanism and utopias: Implications for citizenship education. *Cambridge Journal of Education, 42*(1), 21–35. https://doi.org/10.1080/0305764X.2011.651205

Thapa, A., Cohen, J., Guffey, S. & Higgins-D'Alessandro, A. (2013). A review of school climate research. *Review of Educational Research, 83*(3), 357–385. https://doi.org/10.3102/0034654313483907

Tomaševski, K. (2001). Human rights obligations: Making education available, accessible, acceptable, and adaptable. *Right to Education Primers 3.* Swedish International Development Agency. http://www.right-to-education.org/sites/right-to-education.org/files/resource-attachments/Tomasevski_Primer%203.pdf

UCL Institute of Education. (2021). *Raising refugee children's voices* [Video]. https://youtu.be/aL1OsmRUCiQ

UNESCO. (1990). *World declaration on Education for All and framework for action to meet basic learning needs: Adopted by the World Conference on Education for All: Meeting Basic Learning Needs, Jomtien, Thailand 5–9 March 1990.* https://unesdoc.unesco.org/ark:/48223/pf0000127583

UNESCO. (2000). *The Dakar framework for action: Education for All – meeting our collective commitments (including six regional frameworks for action).* https://unesdoc.unesco.org/ark:/48223/pf0000121147

UNESCO. (2017/18). *Global education monitoring report: Accountability in education – meeting our commitments.* https://en.unesco.org/gem-report/report/2017/accountability-education

UNESCO. (2020). *UNESCO fact sheet on schools rehabilitation in Beirut.* https://en.unesco.org/news/fact-sheet-schools-rehabilitation-beirut-september-17-2020

UNESCO Institute for Statistics. (2019). *Sustainable Development Goals 1 and 4: 4.1.7 Number of years of (a) free and (b) compulsory primary and secondary education guaranteed in legal frameworks.* http://data.uis.unesco.org/index.aspx?queryid=3716

UNESCO, UNDP, UNFPA, UNHCR, UNICEF, UNWOMEN, & World Bank Group. (2015). *Education 2030: Incheon declaration and framework for action. Ensure inclusive and equitable quality education and lifelong learning opportunities for all.* https://unesdoc.unesco.org/ark:/48223/pf0000245656

UNHCR. (2015). *Refugees from Syria: Lebanon – March 2015.* https://reliefweb.int/report/lebanon/refugees-syria-lebanon-march-2015

UNHCR. (2016a). *Lebanon education quarterly dashboard January–March 2016.* https://data.unhcr.org/syrianrefugees/download.php?id=10799

UNHCR. (2016b). *Syrian regional refugee response: Lebanon.* https://data.unhcr.org/syrianrefugees/country.php?id=122

UNHCR. (2019a). *Fact sheet: Lebanon.* https://reliefweb.int/sites/reliefweb.int/files/resources/UNHCR-Lebanon-Operational-fact-sheet-January-2019.pdf

UNHCR. (2019b). *Lebanon: Inter-agency – 2019 LCRP facts and figures – February 2019.* https://data2.unhcr.org/en/documents/details/68104

UNHCR. (2019c). *Lebanon: Education programme.* https://www.unhcr.org/lb/wp-content/uploads/sites/16/2019/04/Education-Factsheet.pdf

UNHCR. (2020a). *Global trends: Forced displacement in 2019.* https://www.unhcr.org/globaltrends2019/

UNHCR. (2020b). *Lebanon crisis response plan 2017–2020: 2020 update*. https://data2.unhcr.org/ en/documents/details/74641

UNHCR. (2023). *Refugee data finder*. https://www.unhcr.org/refugee-statistics/

UNHCR & REACH. (2014). *Barriers to education for Syrian refugee children in Lebanon: Out of school children profiling report*. https://data.unhcr.org/en/documents/details/42462

UNICEF. (2015). *Scaling up quality education provision for Syrian children and children in vulnerable host communities: Report of the sub-regional conference 17–19 June 2014, Amman, Jordan*. UNICEF. https://unesdoc.unesco.org/ark:/48223/pf0000233895.

UNICEF. (2016a). *LCRP – Lebanon crisis response plan 2015–16*. UNICEF. https://data.unhcr.org/ en/documents/details/44246.

UNICEF. (2016b). *Syria crisis education strategic paper: London 2016 Conference*, UNICEF. http:// childrenofsyria.info/wp-content/uploads/2016/01/LONDON-EDUCATION-STRATEGIC-PAP ER-for-website.pdf.

UNICEF & Save the Children. (2012). *Education and rapid needs assessment for displaced Syrian children in schools, community and safe spaces*. https://data2.unhcr.org/en/documents/ download/36499

UNICEF, UNFPA, UNESCO, UNHCR & SCI. (2014). *Situation analysis of youth in Lebanon affected by the Syrian crisis*. UNICEF. https://lebanon.unfpa.org/sites/default/files/pub-pdf/Situation-Analysis-of-the-Youth-in-Lebanon-Affected-by-the-Syrian-Crisis.pdf.

UNICEF, UNHCR, & UNESCO. (2019, March). *Out-of-school-children mapping and profiling 18–19: Findings*. [Paper presentation]. Lebanon Humanitarian INGO Forum.

UNICEF, UNHCR & WFP. (2021). *VASyR 2021: Vulnerability assessment of Syrian refugees in Lebanon*. https://data2.unhcr.org/en/documents/details/90589

United Nations. (1989). *Convention on the Rights of the Child*. https://treaties.un.org/doc/ Treaties/1990/09/19900902%2003-14%20AM/Ch_IV_11p.pdf

United Nations. (2003). *Indicators for monitoring the Millennium Development Goals*. https:// unstats.un.org/unsd/publication/seriesf/seriesf_95e.pdf

United Nations. (2021, 3 September). *Lebanon: Almost three-quarters of the population living in poverty*. https://news.un.org/en/story/2021/09/1099102

UNOCHA (2016) Syrian Arab Republic: key figures. http://www.unocha.org/syria (as of 24 May 2016).

Van Ommering, E. (2019). *Education for peace or war: Everyday interfaces between formal schooling and political conflict in Lebanon* [Doctoral thesis, Vrije Universiteit Amsterdam]. https:// research.vu.nl/ws/portalfiles/portal/93035599/complete+dissertation.pdf

Velasquez, A., West, R., Graham, C. & Osguthorpe, R. (2013). Developing caring relationships in schools: A review of the research on caring and nurturing pedagogies. *Review of Education*, *1*(2), 162–190. https://doi.org/https://doi.org/10.1002/rev3.3014

Virtanen, M., Kivimäki, M., Luopa, P., Vahtera, J., Elovainio, M., Jokela, J. & Pietikäinen, M. (2009). Staff reports of psychosocial climate at school and adolescents' health, truancy and health education in Finland. *European Journal of Public Health*, *19*(5), 554–560. https://doi. org/10.1093/eurpub/ckp032

Ward, C., Bochner, S. & Furnham, A. (2001). *The psychology of culture shock*. Routledge.

Weinstein, H. M., Freedman, S. W. & Hughson, H. (2007). School voices: Challenges facing education systems after identity-based conflicts. *Education, Citizenship and Social Justice*, *2*(1), 41–71.

Wilkinson, J. & Kaukko, M. (2020). Educational leading as pedagogical love: The case for refugee education. *International Journal of Leadership in Education*, *23*(1), 70–85. https://doi.org/ 10.1080/13603124.2019.1629492

World Bank. (2021, 2 April). *Lebanon's economic update: April 2021*. https://www.worldbank.org/ en/country/lebanon/publication/economic-update-april-2021

You, D., Lindt, N., Allen, R., Hansen, C., Beise, J. & Blume, S. (2020). Migrant and displaced children in the age of COVID-19: How the pandemic is impacting them and what can we do to help. *Migration Policy Practice*, *10*(2), 32–39. https://www.unicef.org/media/83546/file/ Migrant-and-displaced-children-in-the-age-of-COVID-19.pdf

Young, M. (2008). From constructivism to realism in the sociology of the curriculum. *Review of Research in Education*, *32*(1), 1–28. https://www.jstor.org/stable/20185111

Index

abuse 34, 38, 55
access 41–2, 54, 56–7, 91, 94,
    99–102, 106, 114, 121, 124–5,
    127, 131–2, 135, 139, 144, 150
accessibility 39, 55, 96
accreditation 40, 56–7
agency 50, 58, 106, 135, 147–150
ambition 9, 63, 67, 79, 86, 88, 92,
    95, 118
appreciation 72, 75, 78, 133
Arabic language 38, 52, 62, 64, 83,
    95, 116, 131
Arsal 6, 46–7, 60–2, 88, 94
art 18, 53–4, 58
authoritarianism 10, 13, 19, 73,
    113, 144, 149

basic education 28–9, 35
Beirut 9, 29, 129–30
belonging 9, 13, 15–16, 18, 20–2,
    24, 41, 50, 58, 60, 67–8, 70–1,
    74–6, 79–80, 83, 86–7, 90,
    94–6, 104–9, 115–17
Beqaa 6, 44, 46–9, 60–3, 88, 94,
    129

care 6, 12, 19–20, 47, 51, 54, 66,
    74, 79, 94, 106, 111–14, 118,
    123, 133, 136, 138–9
citizenship 73, 81, 105
coercion 113–14, 118
collaboration 66, 70–3, 87
community 2, 4, 9, 16–17, 29, 33–5,
    39–41, 46–7, 49–51, 56, 58,
    62, 67–8, 71, 74–5, 80–1, 87–8,
    94–5, 106, 118, 122–3, 134–5,
    143, 149
conflict 2–3, 5, 7–8, 10, 14, 24, 27,
    30–1, 33–4, 36, 41, 49, 51, 57,
    74, 100, 102–3, 144
corruption 30, 129

COVID-19 6, 8–9, 121, 125, 129–31,
    135, 137, 140
critical thinking 34, 57
curriculum 19–20, 34, 37, 40–1,
    51–2, 54–6, 58, 66, 73, 80–2,
    85, 102, 123–4, 127, 135, 137,
    149

dialogic pedagogy 73–4
dialogue 20, 96, 146
dignity 2, 17, 19, 58
displacement 7, 22–3, 31–2, 36, 41,
    48, 60, 99, 102–3, 109, 131,
    148
donor agencies 29–30

economic collapse 30, 42, 121,
    129–30, 137
Education for All (EFA) 27, 35
employment 50, 55
encouragement 78–9, 91
England 2, 6–7, 17, 21, 28, 100–3,
    107
English language 38, 52, 55, 82–3,
    99, 101–2, 109, 112, 116, 124,
    131, 138, 143
equality 14–15, 74, 111, 114, 133
examination 40, 85–6, 104

family 1–2, 17, 22, 32, 35, 60–1,
    70–2, 79, 84, 102–3, 124, 132,
    135
focus group 55–6, 122–31
Fraser, Nancy 8, 13–15, 17,
    21–2, 24, 33, 57–8, 60, 66,
    81, 90, 94, 99, 104, 107–8,
    117, 132
friends 34, 64, 67–72, 83, 86, 109,
    126, 133–4
friendship 63, 73, 124, 126
fun 44, 73, 82–3

9 781800 086814